# IN SEARCH OF

# nixon

# IN SEARCH OF

# nIXon

# A PSYCHOHISTORICAL INQUIRY BY

# BRUCE MAZLISH

BASIC BOOKS, INC., PUBLISHERS

NEW YORK ★ LONDON

© 1972 by Basic Books, Inc.
Library of Congress Catalog Card Number: 71–189669
SBN 465–03219–2
Manufactured in the United States of America
DESIGNED BY THE INKWELL STUDIO

# PREFACE

WITH the explosion of the first atomic bomb at Alamogordo, New Mexico, on July 16, 1945, the office of President of the United States assumed an awesome new importance not only for this country, but also for much of the rest of the world. As the office became more important, so did the person occupying it; and, to stretch the thought further, person quickly becomes personality. Whatever the constraints of the office itself, and they are many and powerful, it has become increasingly clear that many fundamental decisions depend upon the personality of the President of the United States.

The atomic bomb merely dramatized a fact that has become more and more obvious: personality is closely linked to politics and history. The personality of a political leader, moreover, is almost never a mere "accident"; rather, it reflects (though sometimes distortedly) the people who elected him and those who assisted or allowed him to come to power. It tells us a good deal about them as well.

I felt the full force of these general observations during the 1968 Presidential campaign that brought Richard Milhous Nixon to the White House. I was living abroad during the 1968 primaries, and my awareness of the power that inheres in the person of the American President was heightened by reading British and French newspapers and periodicals, by talking to Europeans generally, and by seeing how conscious they were of that power. What I had realized only casually, they recognized explicitly: what America did affected them immensely; what they did affected us peripherally. Continuing discussions with people and political leaders in other nations of our "One World" (at least in destructive, if not constructive potential) confirmed this awareness of how crucial a role America is perceived as playing in their lives. In this respect President Nixon is surely right and not just indulging in political rhetoric when he declares that even his most trivial action has world-wide and historical significance.

This general experience during the 1968 campaign, together with my increasing professional interest in a new branch of history and political science known as psychohistory, convinced me of the importance of a broad psychohistorical study of the future President. Indeed, it seemed to me sufficiently important to warrant an interruption of my own work—on a very different subject—in order to form a "team" to undertake the Presidential project. What more significant task, I asked myself, than to seek greater understanding of the way in which the most powerful man in the world might approach his power and position?

What happened to this original plan, which was to be interdisciplinary, involving people from several different fields? I sounded out five or six outstanding scholars—other historians, political scientists, and psychoanalysts—on their willingness to participate in a "team" inquiry into the psychodynamics of our next President. (This was after Nixon and Humphrey had been nominated, but before the election, and we intended simply to study *whoever* won.) Each of us, using his own set of theories, was to write an analysis of the President; then we would attempt to achieve a group portrait. In addition, we would try to secure alternative "scenarios" of the major problems and events that might confront the President and "predict," as best we could, how he would react to such pressures and opportunities. In order to prevent misuse of our work for political purposes, we would not publish it until *after* the President's term of office. At that time we would compare our analysis and predictions with how things had turned out and, in that light, review the successes and failures of our theories. Obviously, the project was predominantly heuristic.

The estimated funding was only $15,000 to $20,000. We approached a number of foundations and agencies, and their response was the same: The proposed project was most interesting, imaginative, and important, but it was politically inadvisable for those particular foundations to help finance such a study.

I mention this background because it sheds light on the difficulties of doing one kind of interdisciplinary work, psychohistory, in relation to living persons; I am not particularly criticizing the foundations' reactions. (In their place I might have returned the same answer.) This "history" of the aborted project must also stand as a sort of apologia for the present book. Having read, and thought about, a certain amount of material on Richard Nixon, I was loath to discard my work completely. Perhaps, I thought, a sketch might inspire others to further effort. I realize that I am only presenting the beginnings of psychohistory, as a glance by the reader at my remarks on that subject (pp. 151ff.) will show; for one thing almost the entire historical and situational dimension is missing. In fact, what I am offering is primarily a brief psychological sketch of Richard Nixon, informed by an awareness of psychohistorical theory and practice—and a good deal of humility.

In carrying out this task, I have only myself to blame but many others to thank. Some of the themes contained in this book were first explored in a paper presented to The Group for Applied Psychoanalysis (GAP) at a meeting in Boston on January 19, 1970; to the members of that group, I owe much advice and many suggestions. The invitation of a similar group in Buffalo to present my findings also resulted in useful criticism. *The Journal of Interdisciplinary History,* in its Autumn 1970 issue, published substantially the paper presented to GAP; to that journal (especially Miss Stephanie Jones of the editorial staff), its editors, and the M.I.T. Press, who publish the *Journal,* I wish to express thanks for initial editorial assistance. I am deeply in debt to Mrs. Jane Brandford and Mrs. Ruth

Dubois, of my own department of Humanities at M.I.T., for typing the manuscript.

I would also like to thank James David Barber, David Broder, Frederick Sontag, and Dr. Arthur Valenstein for aiding me in various and sundry ways with their thoughts, criticism, and assistance; I am not suggesting in any way that they necessarily support my findings, or even my particular approach. My friends and colleagues, Abraham Zaleznik and Norman Holland, bear a heavier burden: they have worked and toiled with me in the same vineyard of psychohistorical and applied psycho-analytic studies, influencing my thoughts greatly, and thereby sharing to some extent, even if unknowingly, the responsibility for the fruits produced.

My appreciation also goes to Martin Kessler, Vice President and Editorial Director of Basic Books, Inc., the splendid editor of this book, who prodded me constantly to rethink and to re-explain many of my ideas.

Lastly, I wish to thank my wife, Anne, who finally has a book of mine devoid of such forbidding words as *Zeitgeist* and *Weltanschauung,* and who, in turn, has helped me in innumerable ways as I went "in search of Nixon."

BRUCE MAZLISH

*Cambridge, Mass.*
*1972*

# CONTENTS

# 6
# THE PSYCHOHISTORICAL
# APPROACH
## 149

A PORTFOLIO OF PHOTOGRAPHS FOLLOWS PAGE 78

# 1

---

# THE
# NIXON
# PROBLEM

★★★★★★★★★★★★★★★★★★★★★★★★★★★★★★★★★★★★★★★★★★★★

**W**HEN Richard Nixon became the thirty-seventh President of the United States, friends and foes alike conceded that they did not know who the "real" Nixon was, or how he might be expected to behave. Tom Wicker's comment that "the career and personality of Richard Nixon defy confident analysis and what he will do in the White House is by no means easy to divine" accurately reflected the general ignorance and uncertainty.[1]

Wicker, of course, was right, yet the American President is so powerful that "analysis" of his "personality" seems both necessary and justified. To the extent that his personality may affect his decisions and actions, it is our duty to seek the best possible understanding of his character. Most commentators, however, have flitted like moths around this subject. Thus, as Richard H. Rovere correctly points out, "Nixon's leanings, we know, are mostly conservative. But a politician is not a tree that must incline as the twig was bent a long while back." But, having said this, Rovere then undercuts his own observation, remarking that "the greatest and most distressing revelation of this period has been the President's political ineptitude . . . some *kind of perversity* or some failure of calculation seems to make everything go wrong."[2]

Without taking "perversity" too seriously and abandoning Rovere's ambivalence, we can ask: what is the interplay between Nixon's fundamental character traits—the way in which the twig was bent for the *young boy*—and the demands of his situation as a *politician?* To put the matter in more general terms, we can identify the Nixon Problem, highlighting that problem in a series of representative questions.

What in Nixon constantly leads people to search for a "new"

3

(and even a "new, new") Nixon, or a "real Nixon," and to constantly ask, "Has he changed?" "Has he grown and matured as a person as well as a politician?" Why does Nixon seem to experience such personal difficulties in making decisions, and why, when he does make them, are they such unusually "lonely" decisions? Why does Nixon, one of the most tightly self-controlled individuals ever to become President, give way to seemingly unnecessary outbursts, such as his famous "last" press conference of 1962, or to totally unexpected behavior, such as his sudden 1969 night visit to the Lincoln Memorial and subsequent discussion with antiwar students there?

How do we comprehend a Nixon who is almost compulsively concerned with being thought strong and potent, and yet also sees himself as a compassionate and peace-loving person and President? What reconciles these two self-images? How do we understand a Nixon who, on one hand, is a most pragmatic, down-to-earth politician, and, at the same time, a constant daydreamer? How can we best make sense out of Nixon's habit of saying one thing, and then a short while later doing another, without our merely dismissing the question with a brusque, "Oh, but that's how all politicians operate"? Nixon's repeated insistence that allies must consult together, followed by his unilateral decision to go to Peking without first consulting (or even informing) Japan, his fervid denunciation of government control of the wage-price spiral, followed by the dramatic reversal of his New Economic Policy—these examples suggest an unusual division between saying and doing.

What do we say of a Quaker Nixon, dedicated by family tradition to the support of civil rights, who shows himself a determined foe of many federal government measures to hasten integration? How do we understand a Nixon, come to political prominence on the basis of his strong anticommunist beliefs, who then seeks an accommodation with the Russians, and, in a dramatic action that has confounded his own right-wing supporters, an opening to the Chinese Communists?

4

Questions such as these make up the Nixon Problem. One can answer them in part by a political analysis that stays on the surface. For example, in seeking relations with Communist China, Nixon simply bowed to political reality before Peking was admitted to the United Nations. Such answers are valuable and, indeed, fundamental to any further analysis. However, such responses are only partial and must be supplemented by recourse to a "deeper" analysis that includes the personal as well as the political aspect of Richard Nixon. To secure such an analysis, we must turn to the body of theory and fact that concentrates most deeply on this problem: psychoanalysis. In its classic form, however, psychoanalysis is oriented to clinical data about a patient in therapy. In approaching a political subject who is *not* a patient in therapy, it is necessary to bypass orthodox psychoanalysis in favor of a new discipline, variously described as "psychohistory" or "psychological history." Such an approach emphasizes strengths and abilities, creative and adaptive powers, as much as if not more than the usual difficulties pictured in psychotherapy.[3]

Many people are deeply suspicious—and rightly so—of applying psychoanalysis to political figures. There have been some egregious instances of how not to go about this task. For example, the "questionnaire" on Barry Goldwater, addressed to the members of the American Psychiatric Association during the 1964 campaign, which elicited a majority opinion that he was psychologically "unfit" to be President, is a model of irresponsibility. "Treating" Goldwater as if he were a patient, but without the slightest clinical evidence for their conclusions, many psychiatrists simply voted their political prejudices rather than exhibiting their professional competences.

Alas, Freud himself has contributed to the discrediting of psychological history. His book, in collaboration with William Bullitt, on Woodrow Wilson is a sad exemplar.[4] However much one may excuse Freud—he was an old man at the time, morally indebted to Bullitt for helping to rescue his family from the

Nazis—and however much one stresses that Bullitt, in fact, wrote the bulk of the book, the stain on psychological history, though undeserved, is indelible. At the end all one can say is that the book is more psychopathology, and bad psychopathology, than psychohistory, and treat it as a warning example.

Closer to our subject, the effort to cast doubt on Richard Nixon's mental stability by vague accusations that he visited a psychotherapist in the late 1950s has indirectly cast doubt on psychological history. The initial hush-hush handling of the facts showed how *politically* sensitive the effort at *psychoanalytically* understanding a political candidate might be. Without involving ourselves too deeply in Drew Pearson's allegation that Nixon was in therapy for approximately four and one-half years, we can concur with the opinion of one observer that, if the fact were true, "I [would] feel more hopeful about his presidency. When a man has the inner strength to seek competent professional help in finding out more about himself, looks for a way to grow as an individual, tries to improve himself in his own eyes, wants to do something real and constructive about himself as a person . . . then he's on the right track."[5]

As a matter of fact, Nixon himself has a strong distrust of psychiatry. There is a reality factor in his dislike, as well as possibly more personal objections: psychiatric studies *can,* as we have seen, be used as bludgeons to attack a political figure. In the light of our own comments above, we can perhaps sympathize with Nixon's position (without thereby being deterred from our inquiry). In *The Selling of The President, 1968* Joe McGinniss informs us of Mr. Nixon's horror of psychiatrists.

In seeking to "sell the President" panel television shows were worked out for Nixon; inadvertently, on one occasion a psychiatrist was added. McGinniss treats us to the following reaction of Nixon's aides: " 'Jesus Christ,' he [Roger Ailes] said, 'you're not going to believe this but Nixon hates psychiatrists.' 'What?' 'Nixon hates psychiatrists. He's got this thing, apparently. They make him very nervous. You should have heard

Len [Garment] on the phone when I told him I had one on the panel. Did you hear him? If I've ever heard a guy's voice turn white, that was it.' 'Why?' 'He said he didn't want to go into it. But apparently Nixon won't even let one in the same room. Jesus Christ, could you picture him on a live TV show finding out he's being questioned by a shrink?' "[6]

Another account, related by one of Nixon's classmates at Whittier College, suggests that Nixon's scorn for "shrinks" goes back a long way. "One warm spring afternoon in 1933 in a psychology class, Professor Newlin, a senior member of the faculty in his 70's, expounded his theories on the workings of the subconscious mind as related to our reasoning facilities. Dick challenged his synopsis." The classmate then recalls that in the course of his own forty-five minute synopsis, Nixon converted the dear old professor to *his* point of view. (Professor Newlin's reminiscences are not, to my knowledge, on record.)[7]

Whether or not this particular story is apocryphal, the evidence seems abundant that the "introspective" Richard Nixon is not happy with psychiatry and psychiatrists. It is in this context that we must understand his relationship to the physician, or "psychotherapist," whose "competent professional help" is in question, Dr. Arnold A. Hutschnecker.

Our best source of information about that relationship is Dr. Hutschnecker's own article, "The Mental Health of Our Leaders," though it naturally gives a very oblique and indirect picture. In fact, the article is more revealing of Dr. Hutschnecker—a sort of Pavlovian and Freudian synthesizer—than of President Nixon. As the physician who presumably treated Nixon, he clearly had a unique opportunity to try to understand him—as a person, if not as a President. At the very least, then, Nixon's doctor preceded us in the purely psychological side of our study. (Would it not be useful for historians to have *his* record concerning Nixon—to be opened fifty years from now, in order not to violate professional confidence?)

Dr. Hutschnecker, however, is very discreet about his "treatment" of Nixon, and no clear picture of the relationship emerges. Although he had published a book on psychosomatic medicine back in 1951, Dr. Hutschnecker was still, he says, engaged in internal medicine when Nixon consulted him. The doctor's casual reference to a "discussion" in 1955 seems to fix at least that date as part of the consultations, but one cannot even be sure of that. In any case he insists that "during the entire period that I treated Mr. Nixon, I detected no sign of mental illness in him," a comforting if innocuous statement.

In his article Dr. Hutschnecker adopts the Pavlovian classification of four kinds of reactions to stress, or four character types: (1) the strong-excitatory, (2) the lively, (3) the calm imperturbable, and (4) the weak-inhibitory. Or, as he puts it:

Type-one men, who are driven by hostile-aggressive impulses, make up the majority of leaders in all areas of life. Types one and four are the ones most likely to break down under stress. Therefore, they become a risk in social and certainly in political positions of responsibility. Men of type two represent the most desirable leaders because they show a controlled reaction when exposed to stress.

If type one develops emotional maturity and learns to control his aggressive impulses, he can become an aggressive adjusted personality and then make an outstanding type-two leader. (Good examples are Abraham Lincoln and Benjamin Franklin.) The change can take place in a man who may have felt himself driven by ambition but is able to relax after having reached his goal. Type three, passive and dependent, might make a good minor official but not a real leader (President Warren G. Harding and Prime Minister Neville Chamberlain). Type four is weak, inhibited, and, under pressure, has a tendency to withdraw.[8]

How does Dr. Hutschnecker classify Mr. Nixon? Admitting that he had treated Nixon as Vice President, while he was still engaged in the practice of internal medicine, he adds that "naturally, no specific diagnosis can be given even now. What I as a physician am allowed to say is that Mr. Nixon came for physical checkups, none of which showed evidence of any illness." Having disposed of that issue, Dr. Hutschnecker then passes his judgment: "His [Nixon's] behavior indicates that, as President, he may turn out to be a type-two leader, the controlled, adjusted personality." Implicit is the view that at the time he saw him Nixon was a type one, learning to control his aggressive impulses.

Did Dr. Hutschnecker help Nixon, by psychotherapy, in moving from type one to a potential type two? The good doctor, as he should be, is professionally discreet. We may hazard the guess, however, that some psychological guidance, disguised because of Nixon's scorn for psychiatrists, was offered and accepted. Dr. Hutschnecker had authored a book on psychosomatic medicine *before* seeing Nixon. We know that Nixon had serious illnesses in childhood, and that, as one of his Whittier College classmates tells us, "It wasn't uncommon for him to work himself ill."[9] What was more natural than for Nixon to have medical complaints on the borderline of the psychosomatic, and to consult Dr. Hutschnecker? (Knowing that Nixon's father suffered from bleeding ulcers all his life, I would suggest this was the probable presenting symptom, if I had to guess.) In his treatment Dr. Hutschnecker could offer the "psycho," under the guise of the "somatic," to the great benefit of Nixon's development of "inner strength."

Dr. Hutschnecker's therapy seems to have emphasized reassuring Nixon about his strength and goals, and encouraging that side of his personality that tended toward "controlled aggression," that is, peace. In a touching, idealistic statement Dr. Hutschnecker wrote that "I now [1969] believe that if he chooses to resist the military industrial complex, as Eisenhower did, he could become the man to put together, finally, Wendell Willkie's 'one world.' " (We need to remember that in 1940 Nixon voted for Willkie.)

Now, whatever its merits, and I pass no judgment here, Dr. Hutschnecker's particular approach and system is not the one that we shall follow in our inquiry into the "real" Richard Nixon. Dr. Hutschnecker is obviously a man of high moral standards, but his article tells us more about him and his hopes for Nixon than it does about Nixon's psychology.* In this sense it resembles the questionnaire on Goldwater addressed to members of the American Psychiatric Association, or the Freud-Bullitt book on Wilson, and offers us little as a model.

Thus, we shall turn aside from all these limited or faulty approaches and pursue our search for the "real" Richard Nixon through psychohistory. Psychohistory, which has developed from psychoanalysis in the last ten or fifteen years, does, in fact, have some positive work to exhibit. To counterbalance the Freud-Bullitt *Woodrow Wilson,* we can point to the sound, penetrating work of Alexander and Juliette George, *Woodrow Wilson and Colonel House,*[10] which grounds its psychoanalytic insights in solid professional data, giving us a most revealing picture of Wilson, the man and the politician.[11] Erik H. Erikson's contributions, in *Young Man Luther* and *Gandhi's Truth,*

---

* Recently, Dr. Hutschnecker has been in the news again; indeed, he has been made the butt of rather sharp criticism, with his proposal to the White House of what *Newsweek* described as "the mass administration of psychological tests to detect children apt to become anti-social, and even the establishment of special camps for retraining teen-agers." Dr. Hutschnecker is "German-born," as all the news stories carefully pointed out, and there was an unspoken implication in the criticism that what he seeks is some sort of Nazi-type elimination of "misfits." A glance at Dr. Hutschnecker's original article, to which we have been referring here, quickly dispels any such pejorative illusion. His scheme may very well be unrealistic, as its critics point out. But if I understand him correctly, it springs from his dedication to—world peace! In his original Mental Health article, after suggesting that high school and college students be required to undergo psychological testing and that a "kind of mental health certificate" be made "a prerequisite for any job of political responsibility," he advocates the establishment of a separate Department of Peace to "explore the psychodynamics of peace," and to study "the techniques and sublimation of human aggression." His more recent proposals, although addressed to the prevention of crime, hark back to this desire for peace.

Now, whatever else one may think of Dr. Hutschnecker's scheme, it is scarcely heinous. And for President Nixon to wish a sympathetic hearing for his old therapist's dream is hardly sinister.

are brilliant, pioneering efforts to interrelate psychological processes with the political and social currents in which a given
individual finds himself and his identity.[12] Erikson's "identity
crisis" has become one of the clichés of our language. In short,
a psychohistorical study of Richard Nixon does have some valid,
inspiring models upon which to draw.

Psychohistory,* moreover, has advantages denied to other
psychological approaches. For example, psychohistory allows us,
indeed forces us, to take seriously Nixon's role as President.
Many of his decisions will emerge from the demands or constraints of his role rather than of his personality; it is only by
recognizing the former that we can begin to isolate the latter
compulsions. Nixon, whatever his internal dynamics, is not a
patient, but a President functioning in a "real" world. Psychohistory tries to take that fact seriously.

So, too, psychohistory directs our attention to the way in
which Nixon's own personality has been shaped by the values
and institutions of the American society in which he grew up
and now functions; and to the way in which he, as President,
personally reflects, influences, changes, and confirms those
values and institutions. To go in search of Nixon, therefore, is
also to go in search of ourselves.

---

* For a more detailed examination of the psychohistorical approach,
which is vital to the understanding of what we are attempting here, see
Chapter 6, "The Psychohistorical Approach." In fact, for those unfamiliar with or unusually suspicious of psychohistory, it is strongly
recommended that that section be read before the rest of the material on
Nixon.

# 2

---

# FAMILY
# AND
# ROOTS

★★★★★★★★★★★★★★★★★★★★★★★★★★★★★★★★★★★★★★★★★★

THE first thing that strikes an observer is the opaqueness, the nonrevelatory quality of Nixon's life and writings. The blurb writer's claim on the back cover of the 1968 paperback edition of Nixon's book that "Crisis Shapes and Reveals a Man's Character" may be true as a generalization, but requires sharp examination in this case. There is an extraordinary lack of affect about Nixon, and this is not dissipated by the occasional outbreak, such as the 1962 press conference following his gubernatorial defeat. If Nixon did visit Dr. Arnold Hutschnecker as a "psychotherapist," I suspect the going must have been very tough for the doctor. Nixon's opaque quality becomes in itself a subject for investigation; it directs our attention to the time when the young Nixon must have "switched off" his emotions (or was he born with the tendency?). In any case part of the problem labeled "the real Nixon" is rooted in this lack of affect. It certainly adds to the difficulties of our psychohistorical analysis.

One additional comment is useful here. An analyst treating a patient must deal not only with the latter's transferences— the displacement onto him of the patient's feelings toward previous figures—but with his own countertransferences. No less is demanded of the psychohistorian.[1] The general problem of the historian's own bias and involvement with his materials is lifted to another level (or rather, brought to another depth) in psychohistory. But psychohistory has the virtue of compelling one to look as consciously as possible at one's own feelings, as well as at the feelings of one's subject. It is in this spirit that I have sought an understanding of Richard Nixon.

The opaqueness and lack of affect surrounding Nixon seems to fit, both as cause and effect, with the paucity of information about him. For a man who has been as long and as prominently in political life as he has, the lacuna is impressive. For example, Widener Library at Harvard University had only nine or ten items in its catalogue in 1968 (since his election the number has increased; the latest check shows forty-five items, of which two are in German, one in Italian, and one in Spanish), and of these only a few are of any consequence. *Nixon: A Political Portrait,* by Earl Mazo and Stephen Hess, is the 1968 rewrite of Mazo's original 1959 book. It was published, with the 1968 Presidential campaign in mind, by two Nixon partisans (Hess has served in various capacities on Nixon's staff and Mazo is a former *New York Herald Tribune* reporter); however, they made a serious attempt to be nonpartisan. Certainly, at present, it is one of the indispensable sources for any data on Nixon's personal life; Bela Kornitzer's *The Real Nixon* is another useful source.

Since the election Garry Wills' *Nixon Agonistes* has appeared, a fine study of Nixon's ideological significance. Wills adds some biographical data, but he is not attempting to write a life of Richard Nixon. Similarly, Jules Witcover's excellent and interesting book, *The Resurrection of Richard Nixon,* offers tantalizing glimpses of Nixon the man as well as the politician, but only for the years 1962–1967. John Osborne's 1970 and 1971 collections of pieces, *The Nixon Watch,* are also worth mentioning. In addition to these books, a number of articles and interviews concerning Nixon the person have also appeared. While useful (and I have certainly sought to use them), they are in most cases necessarily fragmentary and highly impressionistic, ranging from very good to very bad journalism. In summary, the serious literature on Nixon is still surprisingly sparse, especially that on his life.*

Moreover, caution must be exercised in interpreting any of Nixon's own supposed writings or speeches. As with any Pres-

---

* See Bibliography.

ident, Nixon must resort to speechwriters; indeed, he has a team of them. How, then, can we tell what is "personal" to Nixon? The answer is only partially satisfactory. Nixon himself generally outlines the basic ideas he wants to get across in a particular speech. As William H. Homan describes the procedure in his informative article, "The Men Behind Nixon's Speeches," "Nixon's speeches usually are born in conferences with his writers during which the President-elect outlines his ideas, suggests various sources of information and often cites one or two of his previous statements on a similar theme. The writer assigned then follows up Nixon's leads, tries a draft or two, kicks it around with Keogh [in charge of Nixon's team of speechwriters] and perhaps another writer, and then submits his work to Nixon, who may either discuss further revision with him verbally or write notes in the margins."[2] The speechwriters often coin specific phrases, and veteran Nixon watchers claim to be able to tell which particular writer—Pat Buchanan, the "conservative" or Ray Price, the "liberal," for example— is responsible for which phrase and what kind of style.

Still, in most cases Nixon *has* gone over his speeches and changed them according to his own conception of himself, a conception already shared by his stable of writers. (There was an egregious case during the rush of the 1968 campaign; Nixon delivered a speech, written by a writer he scarcely knew, without having read it before, and with rather unpleasant results. The speech was more demagogic than Nixon wished.) Therefore, most of what he says in formal speeches, if used cautiously, can at best be informative about Nixon the politician.

Fortunately for our particular purposes, however, Nixon likes to write his own speeches more than almost any other President. In most cases there is no secret as to which ones he authored himself. Nixon wrote his own acceptance speech for delivery at the Republican National Convention. Robert Semple informs us that he also wrote his controversial speech in Colorado Springs in June, defending the military and excoriating the "neoisolationists" in Congress, and his stern talk to the students at General Beadle State College in South Dakota, accusing college faculties of fostering student disturbances.[3] These identifiable speeches (again used with appropriate caution) reveal not only Nixon the politician but also Nixon the person.

The one piece of sustained self-revelation that we possess is Nixon's own *Six Crises* (published in 1962, and republished with a new preface in 1968). According to Mark Harris, Nixon wrote only one of the six chapters entirely by himself; in the others he relied on Alvin Moscow to convert his outline into an original draft.[4] The one completely Nixon-authored chapter, "The Campaign of 1960," appears to have been the last, and perhaps the most significant; it makes up more than one-third of the entire book. Although knowledge of Moscow's helping hand colors any interpretation of *Six Crises,* I am proceeding on the assumption that it is still Nixon's most personal revelation.

Even here, however, one must admit that Nixon has sought to reveal as little about himself as possible. As Garry Wills reminds us, "By focusing on a limited number of situations, rather than adopting the standard framework of autobiography, he could omit certain parts of his life entirely. The names of Helen Douglas and Joe McCarthy simply do not occur in the book."[5] Nevertheless, Nixon *does* reveal himself in this book, indirectly as well as directly, almost as much by what he does not tell us (which we know from other sources) as by what he does. To a psychohistorian *Six Crises* speaks in a special language—one not intended by Mr. Nixon.

Serious new research on Nixon's early life is essential, for these sources often raise more questions than they answer, and raise no questions where they should. For example, during World War II Nixon had worked as a lawyer in the OPA for six months. According to Mazo and Hess, "Nixon's six months as a minor government bureaucrat shattered some of his illusions and reshaped a bit of his political philosophy." Entering a "liberal," he emerged a "conservative." What happened during those six months? The experience sounds very important, semitraumatic, yet we are told almost nothing of the personal aspects of this "conversion" episode. The "team" project that I mentioned earlier would have delved into such matters. We shall perforce have to work only with existing materials.

A true psychohistorical account, or even psychobiography, would approach Nixon's life chronologically, seeking to study his personal development in the context of the changing times. As we have suggested, the extant literature is not very conducive to this line of attack. Another possible approach deals with themes or patterns discernible throughout Nixon's life, in the context of general history; I shall take this approach, attending to Nixon's chronological personal development when possible.

Fortunately, both theme and chronology indicate that Nixon's family upbringing should be our first topic. According to Mazo and Hess, "his family intimates see Richard Nixon as a composite of his father, mother, and grandmother."[6] However, we need to see how this "composite" is formed and interrelated. According to Nixon's own account of his grandmother, she "set the standards for the whole family. Honesty, hard work, do your best at all times—humanitarian ideals. She was always taking care of every tramp that came along the road, just like my own mother, too. She had strong feelings about pacifism and very strong feelings on civil liberties. She probably affected me in that respect."[7]

Nixon's mother, Hannah Milhous, was much like his grandmother, a pious Quaker and a strong, hard worker. Clearly, it is from her (and his grandmother) that Nixon has acquired the traits of the "Protestant Ethic" that predominate so forcefully in his makeup. As Nixon's brother Donald recalls, "Dick always planned things out. He didn't do things accidentally . . . he had more of Mother's traits than the rest of us."[8]

19

Richard Nixon was born on January 9, 1913, the second son of Hannah Milhous Nixon. His brother Harold was born four years before him, and after Richard came Donald in 1914, Arthur in 1918, and Edward in 1930. What effect did these siblings have on Richard and on his relations to his mother? The Mazo-Hess account gives only the following data, without interpretation. When the oldest boy Harold contracted tuberculosis, Mrs. Nixon took him to Arizona in hopes of a cure and stayed there for two years. The rest of the family stayed in California, with the boys and their father taking turns preparing the meals. "It was a period of extreme hardship for the whole family." Meanwhile, we are told, "Arthur, the fourth son, became seriously ill, and a week or so later died of tubercular meningitis. He was seven." Worse was to come, for Harold returned from Arizona uncured. One morning, after Richard had driven his brother to town and back home, and then headed off for school, a message came to him, "Come home. Your brother has died."[9]

How old was Richard when his mother "deserted" him? It is extraordinary how difficult it is to determine from the extant literature when, in fact, Nixon's brothers were ill and when, in fact, Nixon himself or his mother was away from home. All that the Mazo-Hess account offers us is the "fact" that Arthur died when he was seven years old, making Richard about twelve or thirteen. Then, we are informed that Nixon at age fourteen spent one summer during the two years his mother and brother Harold were in Prescott, Arizona, putting his nascent oratorical skills to work as a barker at a concession in the Slippery Gulch Rodeo.[10] No date is given for Harold's death, though the stories of Arthur's and Harold's illnesses are run closely together.

However, in James Keogh's *This is Nixon* we are told that Harold got tuberculosis at eighteen and died five years later.[11] An article on "The Young Nixon" in *Life* magazine repeats the fact that Harold died in 1933, aged twenty-three.[12] This would make Richard Nixon about nineteen, though *Life* claims his brother *Don* was nineteen; since Richard was a year older than Don, some confusion persists. Still, Arthur seems to have died in 1925, when Nixon was twelve years old, and Harold in 1933, when Nixon was about nineteen years old.

Besides the vague account given by Mazo-Hess, what confuses this supposedly clear picture is Lloyd Shearer's account of Richard Nixon and Ola-Florence Welch, Nixon's first girl friend—incorporating, as we shall see, a most revealing memoir by her—which reawakens all our lingering doubts. According to Shearer's account:

The oldest Nixon son, Harold, very close to Dick, came down with tuberculosis. Mrs. Nixon took him to Arizona for the dry climate. She helped pay the hospital bills by cooking and scrubbing at the sanitorium. One summer Dick went along. He got a job at a rodeo-carnival in Slippery Gulch, cleaning out stables and such. He did so well that he was promoted to carnival barker. He made an excellent pitchman. During that year, however, his younger brother, Arthur, died of tuberculosis meningitis. And not long after, Harold Nixon also died of tuberculosis.[13]

Such discrepancies in various accounts, and the general air of vagueness in all of them, must give us pause. In addition, the question of when Nixon was *first* separated from his mother must be seen in a new light when we consider the account given by Nixon himself, in an essay about his brother Arthur written when he was seventeen years old. In this essay Nixon informs us that he was first separated from his mother before she took Harold to Arizona. According to Nixon, in 1925, before Arthur took sick, "My aunt had convinced my mother that I should go to her home, several hundred miles away, to continue my study of music."[14] Only after his return home, after the school year was finally ended, did Arthur get sick and die suddenly.

Whatever the discrepancies and difficulties in the reports, however, certain thematic material, useful for psychohistory, emerges. First, if Nixon's account is to be trusted, there is the strong possibility that he unconsciously viewed his being sent away to live with his aunt as some sort of punishment, or lack of real affection on the part of his mother. Next, we may surmise that he unconsciously perceived his beloved mother's leaving him for two years as a betrayal. Consciously, he obviously understood the necessity. (If I am right, this unconscious feeling of "betrayal" might have affected his later attitudes on "traitors" in high places by helping to prepare him emotionally for such a belief.) Whatever the effect, we can be sure of one thing: his mother's absence for two years must have had a crucial impact on young Richard. (Later, I will discuss my suspicion that it turned him back to his father.) We can also postulate that he must have perceived the birth of his brother Donald, only a little over a year after his own birth, as "taking" his mother away from him, thus laying the first seeds of his feelings of the precariousness of life and love. Of course, this perception must have been balanced by the loving concern for all her children that the hard-working, admirable Mrs. Nixon seems to have exhibited.

The death of Nixon's two brothers from some form of tuberculosis is clearly established. What effect did these "traumatic" events have on him? We can speculate on at least two effects. The first is the arousal of strong unconscious guilt feelings. It would be only natural that Richard, the second son, would have rivalrous feelings toward the elder sibling, and an unconscious desire to "replace" him (especially in the affection of the mother); all this would be accompanied by feelings of love toward his brother. We have some evidence of Nixon's feelings in a story he recited while on the campaign trail in 1959. "I remember," he recounted, "that when we were growing up my older brother [Harold] for one year very desperately wanted a pony. My father could have bought it for about seventy-five dollars. And my brother, who died when I was quite young [Would Nixon have considered himself "quite young" at nineteen or twenty? Again the nagging problem of dates] kept saying 'Oh, I want this pony more than anything in the world.' Now, *being the oldest son, he was kind of a favorite* as you can imagine, with my mother and father, and they wanted more than anything else to give him what he wanted."[15] There is double poignancy in this story, unintended by Nixon.

Nixon's account of his feelings toward the life and death of his younger brother Arthur are fortunately available to us in somewhat more extended form. Nixon's school composition, "My Brother, Arthur R. Nixon," referred to earlier, describes his younger brother's short life.[16] Kornitzer believes it reveals "the sincere emotionalism of Nixon's nature." It is not at all clear, however, why Nixon, generally shy and introspective, chose such an intimate subject for public exposition (for which he seems to have received the grade of A—).

"We have a picture in our home," Nixon begins his composition, "which money could not buy." It is a 5″ x 2″ picture of his brother Arthur. The money theme reappears a little further on, when Nixon repeats, "I still say that money could not buy that picture," leaving the reader wondering a bit about the insistence on, and then disclaimer of, the monetary measure (as we shall see later on, at age twelve Nixon had declared he would be a lawyer "who can't be bought"). Is it that Nixon is spurning the temptation, a sort of "negative identity" against which he has been warned, of being willing to "sell" anything, and thus to "sell out" as well? Or is it "merely" a rhetorical device? One suspects a bit of both.

In any case Nixon immediately shifts this part of his account —"But I am starting at the wrong end of my story"—and goes back to 1918 when he was a little boy of five. He recalls how when his father came home and "after talking with my grandmother, who was taking care of my two brothers and me *while Mother was away on a visit* (my italics; again, the mother is away, though this time presumably in the hospital), he came

23

over to where we boys were quarrelling over some toys and told us that there was a little doll over at the hospital for us, a real, live doll!"

The doll story introduces the "girl" theme. Although Richard Nixon and his brothers quickly learned that it was not a "girl doll"—they decided its name should be Arthur, Nixon tells us —it is clear that the parents had wished it were. Discussing his brother's hair, Richard Nixon informs us that "my parents had wanted him to be a girl in the first place; consequently they attempted to make him one as much as possible." Had the parents earlier hoped that Richard and Donald would be girls and conveyed their disappointment subtly? Was Arthur treated specially, as a substitute girl, much to his own resentment, no doubt? Did Richard Nixon, on the one hand, envy his brother the advantages of this position, and, on the other, shun this desire as "weak and sissified," with its implications of passivity and softness. Did he, wishing to affirm his manhood, go to the other extreme of hating girls? We are in the realm of rather murky though interesting speculation. Aside from a few bits and pieces—Nixon's comment about Arthur that "he absolutely would not take interest in anything he thought common to girls"[17] and the information that one of Richard Nixon's favorite topics for debate in early high school days was: "Resolved—Girls are no good"[18]—the information is insufficient.

"Anyway, doll or baby," as Nixon says, when taken to the hospital to see the new arrival, Richard was not impressed. "All I remember about the visit," he writes at seventeen, "was the fact that I was rather disappointed in the baby, because, after all, a tiny baby is not as pretty as a doll. . . ." Next, Nixon claims that "the first two or three years of my baby brother's life are rather indistinct in my memory, for I was engrossed in the first years of my grammar school education." Yet Nixon immediately follows this assertion with some unusually acute observations about his baby brother: for example: "how his eyes changed from their original baby-blue to an almost black shade; how his hair, blond at first, became dark brown; how his mouth, toothless for five months, was filled with tiny, white teeth which, by the way, were exceedingly sharp when applied on soft fingers or toes which happened to get within their reach. . . ."

Such observations hardly seem "indistinct." Nixon must have spent many hours observing his baby brother. Wishing, unconsciously and naturally, to replace *his* older brother Harold, was he concerned, again unconsciously, with the way his beloved younger brother Arthur might "replace" him. Later, sent off to his aunt by his mother, Nixon tells us how "my younger brother was then entering his first year of school [exactly Nixon's situation when Arthur was born?], and learned from letters sent from home that he was doing exceptionally well in all things except drawing [because this was a 'girl's' subject]." Again, feelings of sibling rivalry were likely to be fanned by such letters. However, "the school year ended finally, and my parents came to get me." Arthur, who had missed him, kissed him on the cheek. "I learned later," Nixon recounts, "that he had dutifully asked my mother if it would be proper for him to kiss me, *since I had been away for such a long time.*"[19]

Clearly, Richard Nixon had strong feelings about his brother Arthur. Uppermost would be those of love and devotion; underneath, the natural emotions of sibling rivalry. The sudden and unexpected death of Arthur some weeks after the end of the school year must have come as a crushing event. Problems of "melancholy and mourning," as detailed by Freud in his classic monograph of that name, may have come into play. All sorts of ambivalent and disturbing feelings were undoubtedly called into being. The role of Arthur in Nixon's emotional life was, I believe, crucial and has remained, I suspect, largely unresolved. A therapist, treating Nixon as a patient, would wish to plumb deeply this episode with him.

Therapy, however, is not our purpose here. For our purposes we need only conclude that the death of Richard Nixon's brother Arthur and later of his brother Harold would awaken all the feelings of "survivor guilt"—the guilt and fear-saturated feelings of "I, too, could have died," "I should have died," "I must numb my awareness of actually still being alive, of having survived," and so forth—so well described by analysts such as Robert Lifton.[20] It is not at all clear, however, exactly how in later life Richard Nixon coped with his ambivalent feelings. This subject will arise again when we examine Nixon's relationship with President Eisenhower.

The second effect of his brothers' deaths would be to arouse in him a threat and fear of his own death. We are told by Mazo-Hess that Nixon narrowly escaped death, at age three, in an accident that has left him with a still-existent "ugly scar" (physically hidden "by hair always parted on the right"). "Nixon," they continue, "has always been susceptible to illness of one kind or another since that childhood experience. When he was four he nearly died of pneumonia."[21] More than with most children, then, we can assume a death anxiety in Nixon, accentuated by the actual deaths of his younger and older brothers. Death seemed to have lingered as a constant presence in the Nixon house, and it is significant that many years later Nixon recalled in detail that "the downstairs bedroom off the living room was where two of my brothers died."[22] Even more to the point is the recollection of Ola-Florence Welch, Richard Nixon's first girl friend, who remarked concerning the deaths of Arthur and Harold that "Dick was kind of fatalistic. He thought he might get TB too."[23] Obviously, the threat of death was constantly present in Richard Nixon's psyche. Therefore, it may be that Nixon's need for "crises" is partly motivated by the need to confront his death fears, repeatedly and constantly.

The paucity of our information leaves us only with these speculations: a possible sense of betrayal by the beloved mother; guilt over death wishes; and anxiety over death fears. Out of these feelings Richard Nixon could draw either strengths or weaknesses, or both.

We have talked about the mother and the brothers. What about the father? Here the picture seems even more complicated. Francis (Frank) Nixon seems to have been a good man in a family dominated by strong women. In spite of his efforts, however, he seems also to have been a "failure," who drifted from enterprise to enterprise: a Black Irishman, given to black moods, the American who did not "make it rich." Frank Nixon first emigrated to Whittier, California for reasons of health, having suffered severe frostbite while running an open trolley in Columbus, Ohio. When he met Hannah Milhous in 1908 in southern California, he was still the motorman of a trolley. Since grandmother Milhous, we are told, had "a big house on the boulevard," we can assume that Frank Nixon had married above his station. In any case he tried to improve himself. Speculating that Whittier would grow rapidly, he opened a gasoline station (in 1922, moving from nearby Yorba Linda, where Richard was born, to Whittier proper; in Yorba Linda Frank Nixon had planted a lemon grove that failed). He also converted an abandoned meeting house nearby into a general store (where Richard worked at the counter and pumped gas as well). In none of these enterprises did he seem to have great success. As one commentator puts it, the elder Nixon was "a rolling stone and man of many jobs."

My theory is that Richard Nixon, who so resembled his mother in her traits of hard work and persistence, eventually turned those traits to use in terms of an *identification* with the father. We catch the flavor of some of that identification—almost a mimicry—when we learn that Frank Nixon "had a keen distaste for writers and newspapermen,"[24] and when Donald tells us that "any time there was a campaign on, my father was involved. There was nothing he liked better than to argue. He'd take either side." [25]

More importantly, in his identification Nixon also sought to redeem his father by being successful. I suspect that the full identification took place shortly after what I have called the mother's "betrayal," around age twelve or thirteen, when young Richard would have been moving into the swift currents of feelings that we call the reawakened Oedipus complex. All in all, he seems to have navigated these currents with relative success, being able to "let go" of his mother and to take on the role of his father. In so doing, he also had to accept the need to go beyond his father's abilities and capacities, and to avoid those parts of his father's character that had led to failure. Thus, there were negative as well as positive features to the identification. There was, moreover, a price to be paid for the identification with his father; Nixon must always have been haunted by the fear that he, too, might fail.

What is the evidence to back up such speculation? Mazo and Hess tell us how Richard's father served as an inspiration for his decision to become a lawyer and to enter politics. Incensed by the Teapot Dome Scandal, Frank Nixon "became increasingly livid over each new disclosure in the sensational theft of government oil reserves through the connivance of principles [*sic*] in President Harding's administration. His diatribes against 'crooked politicians' and 'crooked lawyers' dominated the family conversation for weeks and provoked 12-year-old Richard to abandon the romance of railroading for a more idealized road to greatness. His mother was the first to be told of the decision. She recalls that the boy declared 'I will be an old-fashioned kind of lawyer, a lawyer who can't be bought.' [Incidentally, it is worth noting the stress on "old fashioned"—an acceptance of his father's world, rather than the modern one—and the significance of "lawyer" as a temporary midpoint between his mother's desire for him to be a preacher and his father's interest in politics.] Donald, the third Nixon boy and Richard's junior by two years, believes his brother 'made up his mind to political life then and there, whether he realized it or not.' "[26] From our vantage point we can also see that the father's diatribes against "crooked politicians" corresponds closely to the mature Richard Nixon's attacks on "corruption."

More convincing than the various biographical accounts are Richard Nixon's own statements in *Six Crises*. Noting that "the last thing my mother, a devout Quaker, wanted me to do was to go into the *warfare of politics,*"[27]* Nixon explains that there were "two major reasons for my competitive drive. . . ." One was economic (the necessity to win a scholarship in order to go to college), the other personal:

The personal factor was contributed by my father. Because of illness in his family he had had to leave school after only six years of formal education. Never a day went by when he did not tell me and my four brothers how fortunate we were to be able to go to school. I was determined not to let him down. My biggest thrill in those years was to see the light in his eyes when I brought home a good report card. He loved the excitement and the battles of political life. During the two years he was bedridden before his death (which came just at the start of the 1956 campaign) his one request of me was that I send him the *Congressional Record*. He used to read it daily, cover-to-cover, something I never had the patience to do. I have often thought that with his fierce competitive drive and his intense interest in political issues, he might have been more successful than I in political life had he had the opportunity to continue his education.[28]

In many ways this is perhaps the most revealing of Nixon's rare revelations in *Six Crises*. We have honest affect. Let us analyze the passage further. "I was determined not to let him down." Here we have Nixon redeeming his unsuccessful father. There are also strong guilt feelings in this account. The father awakens guilt in his sons by telling them how fortunate they are to have what he did *not* have: education. Yet Richard can overcome this guilt (and the resentment he must have felt at the accusation), as well as the natural guilt at doing better than his father, by offering excuses for the latter's failure. Frank Nixon had had to leave school because of family illness, and

* Richard Nixon, *Six Crises* (New York: Doubleday, 1968). Quoted with the permission of Doubleday & Co. and W. H. Allen & Co.

*this* had kept him from being successful.* Moreover, Nixon concludes that *if* his father had had the same educational opportunities as he, Richard, did, his fierce competitive "drive and interest" in political issues would have made him even more successful than the future President of the United States. Hence, Nixon was not really displacing and surpassing his father— the dangerous fantasied Oedipal victory—but, by identification with him, merely doing in his person what his father (given the opportunities) would also have accomplished. As a result, Nixon could, with a good heart, follow his father, forsaking his mother in this crucial matter, into the "warfare of politics."

As we have noted, Hannah Milhous was a dedicated Quaker, strongly pacifist. Her psychological dominance over her husband manifested itself here, too, it would seem; he gave up his forebears' "Bible-pounding" Methodism and upon marriage embraced her faith. The children were all raised as Quakers, which greatly influenced Richard Nixon's life. His attitudes toward political "warfare" and feelings about aggressive impulses were obviously influenced by his religious background; so were many of his friendships and personal relations.

Initially, Nixon was most influenced by his mother's version of Quakerism, presumably akin in its idealism and pacificism to that found among Philadelphia Quakers. Gradually, it appears, he swung over to his father's watered-down version,

---

* In reality it appears that Frank Nixon did not have to leave school, but did so out of boredom and a desire to make his fortune (See Wills, *Nixon Agonistes,* p. 177). It is also interesting to note that Frank Nixon's mother died when he was seven; could it be that Richard Nixon's feelings of maternal "desertion" were overdetermined by accounts of his father's experience? (Cf. Costello, *Facts about Nixon,* p. 19). Finally, we may note a typical American notion propagated by Frank Nixon, as reported by his son. Thus, Richard Nixon tells us, "I want a life, as my Dad used to tell me when we were growing up, that is better for my children than I've had myself." (Theodore White, *The Making of a President, 1960* (New York, 1961), p. 307.)

which corresponded much more closely to the "informality and emotionalism" of the frontier Quakerism generally to be found in California.[29] In this form it was hardly distinguishable from a sort of fundamentalism. Interestingly enough, Nixon, in a conversion episode at which his mother was not present, definitely cast his lot with his father's reversion to "Bible-pounding." The day after he entered high school, his father took him and his two brothers to Los Angeles to attend the revival meetings conducted by the Chicago evangelist, Dr. Paul Rader. As Nixon tells it, "We joined hundreds of others that night in making our personal commitments to Christ and Christian service."

Nixon revealed this episode (unmentioned by Mazo and Hess) in the November 1962 issue of Billy Graham's monthly magazine, *Decision,* thus demonstrating that his fundamentalist "commitment" still held. Such a commitment would drastically color not only Nixon's emotional life, but also his cognitive beliefs.* That Billy Graham was Nixon's first preacher in the White House, that he preached at the funeral of Nixon's mother, Hannah, in 1967 (had she changed her views? would she have approved?), that Nixon was one of the original sponsors for his 1965 New York rally, and that Nixon has appeared at a number of Graham rallies, including the grand finale of one of his recent New York "crusades," are all facts that support this contention.

Yet Nixon in general has not worn his religion on his sleeve, perhaps owing to his general fear of revealing his intimate

---

* Parenthetically, we ought to note with Wills that *all* of the contenders for the Republican nomination in 1968 "had fundamentalist backgrounds—strict Baptist for Rockefeller, Mormon for Romney, Christian Scientist for Percy, Quaker for Nixon, Goldwaterism [a religion, or is Wills being humorous?] for Reagan. In fact, most had been, at one time or another, lay preachers." (Wills, *Nixon Agonistes,* p. 31). This fact certainly tells us something important about the Republican party; and from a psychohistorical viewpoint something even more important about American politicians and the American electorate!

feelings. Although we are told that as a boy "he and his family attended one form of service or another four times on Sunday and several times during the week,"[30] the mature Nixon, at least before becoming President, did not attend church regularly. Nor, if we judge by his account in *Six Crises,* does religion seem to have played a role, except as a general ethical inspiration, during his crucial encounters. In short, Richard Nixon is not outwardly a deeply religious man. Even his White House services seem social occasions, devoid of true religious piety.

Only once so far during his Presidency has there been an exception to Nixon's rule of no outward display of religious conviction. On April 3, 1971, Nixon issued a statement on abortion (in the armed forces), declaring that he was reversing previous policy and that henceforth military bases would obey state laws in this matter rather than act on a federal mandate. Instead of resting his case on "local government" as he might easily have done, Nixon went out of his way to declare that "the country has a right to know my personal views." I quote his declaration at length:

From personal and religious beliefs I consider abortions an unacceptable form of population control. Further, unrestricted abortion policies, or abortion on demand, I cannot square with my personal belief in the sanctity of human life—including the life of the yet unborn. For surely the unborn have rights also, recognized in law, recognized even in principles expounded by the United Nations.

Ours is a nation with a Judeo-Christian heritage. It is also a nation with serious social problems—problems of malnutrition, of broken homes, of poverty and of delinquency. But none of these problems justifies such a solution.

A good and generous people will not opt, in my view, for this kind of alternative to its social dilemmas. Rather, it will open its hearts and homes to the unwanted children of its own, as it has done for the unwanted millions of other lands.

Were Nixon's "religious beliefs" derived from his formal Quakerism? The actual Quaker position on abortion, as given in a report, *Who Shall Live?* prepared for and circulated by the

American Friends Service Committee, reads, "We believe that no woman should be forced to bear an unwanted child. A woman should be able to have an abortion legally if she has decided that this is the only solution she can accept and if the physician agrees. . . ."[31] Was Nixon simply appealing to Catholic voters? The matter seems deeper and more personal than that, to warrant this unusual self-revelation by Nixon. Why the stress on "unwanted children?" Does the idea of abortion somehow touch on Nixon's childish death fears, which we discussed earlier?

In any case can we say anything more about the inward significance of his religious training and convictions? We have almost no data. However, in an interview with Wills Nixon himself discussed the effect of his Quakerism. "Oh, I suppose it is the stress on privacy. Friends believe in doing 'their own thing,' not making a display of religion. That's why I never use God's name in speeches, or quote the Bible." Then, in an admirable self-insight Nixon added, "I suppose the Quakerism just strengthened my own temperament here. I'm an introvert in an extrovert profession."[32] Wills claims that much of Nixon's admiration for Woodrow Wilson stems from the fact that Nixon "is a fundamentalist on domestic values" and "holds to the moral framework of American thought about foreign affairs," [33] thereby emulating his strict Calvinist predecessor in the Presidency.

For our purposes, however, there may be an even more important consideration. I would suggest that the little material we have on the subject allows us to postulate a significant attitude toward authority (along with the ambivalence to aggressive impulses mentioned earlier) emerging from Nixon's religious background.

Our clue comes from his relationship with and approval of Billy Graham. Graham's views on "authority" are apparent in such quotations as: "Man rebelled against God, and so he was separated from God by sin," and "The human race was made for the control of God, and young people are made for the control of their parents."[34] In a speech to an organization of Protestant policemen in New York, paraphrasing a section from Romans 13 on the obligation to submit to authority (and substituting the word "policeman" for "authorities"), he declared that "the Bible teaches that the policeman is an agent and servant of God, and the authority that he has is given to him not only by the city and the state but is given to him by Almighty God."[35]

I am not suggesting that Nixon and Graham are totally alike, although there are a number of unusual similarities in their background. Both came from deeply religious families, with the mother being most devout; both had fathers (Graham's, though named William Franklin Graham, Sr., was also known as "Frank") who had less education and "breeding" than their wives and sons; both had "conversion" episodes in their high school years. The key difference seems to be that Billy Graham strenuously rebelled in his early years and, then, in adolescence gave in *completely* to "God the Father." Nixon neither rebelled nor, as a result, bowed so totally before authority. In fact, it seems that he never questioned it. (Or has all the data on his rebellion simply been passed over in silence?)

One curious line in the Mazo-Hess account further relates to this problem of attitude toward authority. "Richard," they tell us, "took his spankings without a whimper."[36] I would certainly have passed by this line without a second thought— after all, parents were less inhibited about physical punishment in Nixon's generation—except for my attention being drawn to the role of whippings in Graham's life. Autobiographical information about Graham is filled with stories of the harsh whippings given him by his father. "If I broke a rule," Graham reports, "believe me, Father never hesitated. Off came his belt. Mother preferred a long hickory switch. I had literally hundreds of whippings until I was thirteen or fourteen."[37] Billy Graham's powerful spirit and physique ultimately buckled to the "rightness" of punishing authority.

What of Nixon? Was he at any time a rebellious child who needed repeated spankings? Who exercised this "authority," his father or mother? Until what age? We are given the impression that Nixon's "tussle" with authority was never at any point traumatic. He simply accepted the structure of things as they were. But we cannot be sure. All that we have is general agreement that the father, Frank Nixon, was given to fits of anger and irritability and spanked his sons. Whether Hannah also spanked them is unclear, though doing so would seem out of character for her. Whether his father actually whipped Richard is also unclear, as the following passages from Kornitzer indicate: "Frank's rigid and uncompromising attitude, not only toward politics but toward life in general, made life hard for his family. 'He would not hesitate using the strap or rod on the boys when they did wrong,' Hannah says, 'although I don't remember that he ever spanked Richard.'" When asked directly, Richard Nixon told Kornitzer, " 'Dad played no favorites with us . . . when you got into mischief, you had to be pretty convincing to avoid punishment. . . . He had a hot temper, and I learned early that the only way to deal with him was to abide by the rules he laid down. Otherwise, I would probably have felt the touch of a ruler or the strap as my brothers did.' "[38]

Whatever the actual reality of the spankings, I am suggesting that their "psychic reality," plus Nixon's Quaker fundamentalist religious background, is undoubtedly important in explaining his attitude toward authority, though it must be placed in the context of his family's general mode of upbringing. While the picture is shadowy, we seem to see the outlines of a fairly placid development, with an easy and unrebellious identification with the father, and thus authority. Such an attitude, for example, must have helped Nixon to survive his relations with Eisenhower and to emerge at the time of the Checkers Speech still saying, "What had happened during the past week had not shaken my faith in Eisenhower."

Nixon's Quakerism also figures dramatically in the Hiss case, which first brought him to prominence. In *Six Crises* Nixon tells us that he became convinced that Chambers was telling the truth when the following incident occurred. "I happened to mention the fact," Nixon tells us (but without telling us why he mentioned this particular fact),

that I was a member of the Society of Friends. He said that he and his family attended the Friends' meeting in Westminster. He recalled that Mrs. Hiss, at the time he knew her, also had been a Friend.

Then his eyes lit up, he snapped his fingers, and he said, "That reminds me of something. Priscilla often used the plain speech in talking to Alger at home."

I knew from personal experience that my mother never used the plain speech in public but did use it in talking with her sisters and her mother in the privacy of our home. Again I recognized that someone else who knew Priscilla Hiss could have informed Chambers of this habit of hers. But the way he told me about it, rather than what he said, again gave me an intuitive feeling that he was speaking from first-hand rather than second-hand knowledge.[39]

The coincidence of so many Quakers in the Hiss case is rather extraordinary, given the rarity of Quakers in the United States (120,000 according to *The New York Times*). I cannot help suspecting that one factor explaining the intensity of Nixon's involvement in the case was his partial identification with Chambers, against Alger Hiss, the insolent representative of the Eastern Establishment (on pp. 36–44, we shall investigate Nixon's ambivalence toward it). Thus, Nixon describes Chambers as "a thoughtful, introspective man, careful with his words, speaking with what sounded like the ring of truth";[40] he adds, "like most men of quality, he made a deeper impression personally than he did in public."[41] This sounds much like Nixon's vision of himself. In any event, in defending Chambers' "truthfulness," Nixon was attesting to his own belief in his Quaker past—and thus his own "truthfulness."

The setting in which family and religion exercised their influence on Nixon was rural Californian. The attraction of the big city and the East became the counterpull to his life; throughout, I believe, he manifested great ambivalence. In this he mirrored the attitude of many of his fellow Americans.

The farming village in which Nixon was born, Yorba Linda, was about thirty miles inland from Los Angeles. Whittier, where he moved when he was about nine, was thirteen miles from Los Angeles. By 1937, when Nixon returned to Whittier to practice law, it had become a suburb of Los Angeles, with a population of about 25,000. According to Mazo and Hess, at that time "Nixon confided to a few intimates that he aimed sooner or later to get into a big city law practice."[42]

Nixon's goal was not simply a "big city law practice"; it was really an Eastern city law practice. After graduation from Duke Law School, Nixon and two fellow seniors went job-hunting in New York. "They applied at practically all the well-known law offices," we are told. Nixon's "highest hope was to find a place with Sullivan and Cromwell, where John Foster Dulles was a senior partner. Nixon recalls, however, that he was attracted more by the 'thick, luxurious carpets and the fine oak paneling' of the Sullivan and Cromwell reception room than by the possibility of being a low-echelon associate of Dulles. 'If they had given me a job,' he said in 1958, 'I'm sure I would have been there today, a corporation lawyer instead of Vice-President.' "[43]

Nixon's two friends landed New York jobs, one with a distinguished law firm, and the other with a large oil corporation. Nixon got no offers from any of the firms to which he had applied. Then, after waiting for an FBI job that did not materialize, Nixon returned to Whittier to practice law. Nixon clearly had not made it on his first try. Psychologically, he must have perceived himself as a failure, like his father. There was, therefore, much to atone for when he finally succeeded in his initial ambition, to be a big corporation lawyer, and took his place in 1963 as a senior partner in the Wall Street firm of Mudge, Stern. Ironically, it was only through his second choice, politics, that Nixon realized his boyhood dream.

Rural versus urban, this has been a perennial tension in American political life. Nixon (like his wife, Pat) was a "farm boy" who made good in the city. Yet the values that he started with, and that are strongest in him, are rural (Protestant) values, and it is these that he brings into confrontation with his urban desires. This ambivalence (it reminds one in many ways of Henry Ford, who wished his workers to have little farms attached to their houses, at the same time as he pioneered assembly-line techniques and contributed to the growth of Detroit) is still present in Nixon's acceptance speech of 1968, when he says, "I see a day when life in rural America attracts people to the country, rather than driving them away." [44]

For Nixon, of course, rural really means small town—a Yorba Linda or Whittier. He was telling the truth, as well as being cleverly political, when at the dedication of the Karl E. Mundt Library at General Beadle State College, Madison, South Dakota (June 3, 1969), he began with, "I feel at home here because I, too, grew up in a small town." And it was in Deshler, Ohio, a town of about 2,000, that Nixon noticed a young girl holding a sign saying "Bring Us Together," which was to become Nixon's 1968 campaign slogan. Theodore White gives the context of this decision. "The people in the crowds were so much older than in 1960, said Nixon—The young people must be leaving the farms and small towns, they were going to the cities. He had noticed that [he told Bob Finch]. A lot of thinking had to be done about this after the election, he concluded. Deshler recurred to Nixon again, still later. Through his 'closed eyes that evening he had, apparently, seen a young girl somewhere in the crowd holding up a sign that few of us saw. BRING US TOGETHER, it read."[45] On one level this simply meant to unite the country. On another it represented the political necessity of Nixon's position in the Republican party after the 1964 debate on Goldwater had split the party wide open. On still another level, I am suggesting, it embodied Nixon's effort to "bring together" the small town and the big city. And, on a still deeper level, I believe, it represented symbolically his own attempt to deal with divisions within himself —a boy who had left the farm and small town and gone to the city.

Nixon was not only a small town boy, he was also a "Westerner" who finally made good in the East. He not only made good, but he actively bowed to the pieties of Eastern success by sending his daughters to Finch and to Smith College and presenting them to society in a Debutante Ball (one result being their marrying boys from well-known families), and by himself joining prestigious New York men's clubs such as the Metropolitan and the Links.

Yet ambivalence about the Eastern Establishment undoubtedly runs deep in Nixon (as it did, incidentally, in Eisenhower). We have already seen how he had wished to enter an Eastern Establishment law firm and had been rejected. The rejection was to continue in numerous and sometimes subtle ways. "Desiring above all," Theodore White tells us in 1960, "to be liked and accepted by the Eastern world which had always seemed so strange to him, he could make no behavior or speech of the 'new Nixon' acceptable to the liberals. 'The trouble with Dick,' said one of his friends, 'is that he's been brainwashed by the Eastern liberals. If he lives to be a hundred, he'll never forget that Herblock cartoon of the welcoming committee, and him climbing out of the sewer to greet it, all covered with that stubby beard of his.' "[46] Nor, presumably, could Nixon ever forget that in 1952 it was his "friends" in the Eastern Establishment who led the movement to get Eisenhower to drop him as the Vice Presidential candidate.

By 1968, however, Nixon had managed not only to break into the Eastern Establishment, but to beat it at its own game. Now at last he could "reject" it and satisfy his own deep feelings of humiliation. Note, for example, that Nixon's business friends are mainly "new" men, newly rich, self-made: a Donald Kendall of Pepsi-Cola or a Robert Abplanalp, the aerosol valve industrialist, rather than a Rockefeller or a Loeb.

Garry Wills has described Nixon as "the right man for a period of resentment."[47] There is a special "fit" between Nixon's own personal resentments and those of the American electorate whom he has called "the Forgotten American" (borrowing the phrase from one of Goldwater's talks in 1961). Strange as it may seem, Nixon, the protagonist of the party of big business, whose campaign strategy meetings often took place at the posh New York Metropolitan Club, embodies strong "populist" elements.

Populism (and I speak of a general attitude, not of the specific Populist party of 1892 and its program) often tends to anti-intellectualism, antiurbanism, anticentralization, and anti-Eastern elitism; it is also frequently anti-big business. Nixon, of course, is not opposed to big business, although he has tried to identify with the "hardhats" of America, but he does share some of the other elements characteristic of populism. To take but one example, though in some moods Nixon prides himself on being an intellectual, his attitude is typically ambivalent, and he also exhibits strong anti-intellectual attitudes. As Wills points out, this trait goes back at least to his college days; moreover, "His uneasiness with brilliance he maintains to this day—the feelings that burst out when he talks about 'intellectuals' . . ."[48] Yet if we remind ourselves that one of Nixon's youthful heroes was Robert LaFollette (again Nixon followed his father in this matter), the strangeness of his "populism" partly disappears.

In 1968 Nixon's personal resentment and his populist streak also fitted in with the supposed requirements of Republican strategy. Announced back in 1964 as Goldwater's "Southern

Strategy," it assumed, in the words of one of its proponents, William Rusher, that "the Republican strategy needs refiguring." The party, Rusher added, must be "given a chance to break into this bloc [Southern states] once denied them—that alone would make the Eastern states less vital."[49] By 1968 Nixon had made this strategy his own, dressed out in the elegant psephological language of John Mitchell's aide, Kevin Phillips. "Who," Phillips had written, "needs Manhattan when we can get the electoral votes of eleven Southern states? Put those together with the Farm Belt and the Rocky Mountains and we don't need the big cities."*

As in so many other areas, Nixon has ambivalent feelings about the Southern Strategy, the East, and "big cities." Yet in this case his ambivalence could be pleasantly, if only temporarily, resolved by the political necessity of his time and party. In psychohistorical terms we have here a nice instance of what can best be referred to as a "corresponding process." What for another candidate might have been mere external political necessity becomes for Nixon a matter of intense personal need as well; and the "sincerity" of his feelings is intuitively felt by his followers. It is a fine fit.

Let us now go back in Nixon's career to an earlier time and examine the role that this ambivalence toward the Eastern Establishment played in one of his first major political "crises." Some of this general feeling must have been present in the encounter with Alger Hiss, who was everything Nixon was not: in

---

* There is a nice irony to such statements, paraphrasing as they do the antiurban sentiments and strategy of the Chinese Communists, voiced by Lin Piao in his famous 1965 speech, "Long Live the Victory of the People's War," where he declared that the rural nations were bound to defeat the urban nations in the course of the world revolution. "Taking the entire globe, if North America and Western Europe can be called 'the cities of the world' then Asia, Africa, and Latin America constitute the rural areas of the world,' " Lin Piao announced; and in this version of the "southern strategy," he prophesied that the rural areas were "scientifically" predetermined for victory.

Nixon's own words Hiss (the name is perfect for its ambivalent conjoining of Horatio Alger, the Nixon hero, and "hissing" the villainous Easterner) "had come from a fine family, had made an outstanding record at Johns Hopkins and Harvard Law, had been honored by being selected for the staff of a great justice of the Supreme Court,"[50] and so forth. Hiss, the embodiment of Eastern values, treated Nixon, the thirty-five-year old freshman Congressman, like dirt. Nixon's chapter on the Hiss Case is filled with statements about Hiss, such as: "His manner was coldly courteous and, at times, almost condescending";[51] "He was rather insolent toward me";[52] and "his manner and tone were insulting in the extreme."[53] If I am right that there was a partial identification with his fellow "failed" Quaker, Chambers, then the scorned Nixon's feelings must have been doubly outraged by the patrician Hiss. Obviously, Nixon had straightforward legal and political reasons for attacking Hiss as he did; I am only suggesting that the passion and tenaciousness came from deeper sources.

There is a strange irony in the fact that in the end Nixon, a product of the West who remained deeply suspicious of the East, was rejected by his own state of California, in his traumatic defeat for governor in 1962 (and largely on the grounds that he had deserted California and its interests for larger, more Eastern-oriented spheres). Only after finally succeeding in the East was he able to mount his winning Presidential campaign.

To understand Nixon fully, one would need carefully to analyze the turbulent currents of California life, values, and politics. Its mixed Republican-Democratic politics, the evangelicalism in Los Angeles, the extremes of right-wing Birchites and left-wing Bohemians, all of this and more have shaped Richard Nixon's perceptions and feelings.[54] In many ways Nixon is a "typical" southern Californian, but with a heightened ambivalence toward the Eastern Establishment.

One wonders, therefore, at the significance of Nixon's acquisition, as President, of a luxurious house in San Clemente, California. In this heavily Birchite county, in the exclusive Cyprus Shore community, Nixon bought a ten-room house and five acres for $340,000. Did he, figuratively speaking, finally return "home," successful? It is interesting to note that his house is only four miles away from his favorite restaurant at San Juan Capistrano where, we are told, "he dines at least once each time he comes home. It is a setting that evokes memories for the President and First Lady who dined there during their dating days thirty years ago." It is interesting, too, that there is a railroad track along the beach, below the house, "on which six trains pass daily between Los Angeles to San Diego to the South."[55] Does it remind the President of his boyhood dreams, associated with the Santa Fe Railroad line that ran past his house in Yorba Linda? As Mazo and Hess describe it, "Long freight trains rumbled past at all hours. The Nixon homestead shook and the throbbing stirred in Richard visions of faraway places."[56]

San Clemente aside, Nixon seems the prototypic rootless, homeless American, or rather, the twentieth-century version of the frontier-moving American, now roaming up and down the countryside in mobile homes (Nixon simply has many "homes" to which he moves). The railroad was merely his first dream vehicle. His aunt, Mrs. Olive Marshburn, recalls how "there was a good friend of the family from Indiana who was a Santa Fe engineer. He lived in Needles. But he would come to visit Frank, and tell the boys about his work and travel. Richard was fascinated."[57] As Wills perceptively points out, from Whittier railroad tracks could only lead East, and Nixon marks the reverse movement of that frontier tide, ebbing to its limits. Young Richard Nixon gave up his early dream of being a railroad engineer in order to become a lawyer-politician. In his new vocation, however, Nixon could still travel up and down the country in trains.

Nixon also "moved" with the times, and planes soon replaced trains. By November 1969, after one year as President,

Nixon had, according to the Republican National Commmittee, already logged in Air Force One, "a total of 75,443 air miles since taking office—already three times more than the previous holder, Lyndon B. Johnson."[58] If we recall that Nixon flew 5,000 miles for a brief appearance at an Apollo splashdown in the Pacific, we can well believe Nixon's record-making flight capacity. Nixon is the essential American, always "on the move," both socially and geographically. The incessant movement clearly serves some deep need in Nixon, rooted as it is in his childhood dreams of being a railroad engineer and traveling to faraway places. It is also, of course, politically and socially functional for a politician.

Almost all observers have noted Nixon's lack of "place." Back in 1960 Theodore White wrote of Nixon that "his campaign had been based on home talk. But he had no real home except where his wife was; he was a stranger, even . . . in California, seeking home and friendship."[59] By 1968, in the face of a victorious Presidential campaign, White amended his view to read, "he had long since ceased to be a Californian; he had never, really, been a New Yorker; his home place, truly, was Washington. And so now Richard Nixon was preparing to go home."[60]

Washington as "home," however, must be seen in a special light. As Robert Semple has pointed out, "Mr. Nixon's visits to the Western White House [San Clemente] are advertised as a useful antidote to the notion that the East in general and Washington in particular are the true centers of power. 'The San Clemente operation gives Westerners a symbolic share in the business of Government,' Herb Klein once told a reporter, 'pulling West closer to East and unifying the nation.' "[61] San Clemente, then, has real political as well as psychological significance. We are concentrating on the way in which the political and psychological interact and form part of what earlier we described as corresponding processes. In a sense Washington is "home" for any politician of national stature. San Clemente is very special for Richard Nixon. It represents in a large part *his* rejection of the Eastern Establishment, and a return home of sorts, in a time and country where, as Thomas Wolfe put it, "You Can't Go Home Again."

Yet his comparable house in Key Biscayne, Florida, must check this thesis and remind us that Nixon still retains his ambivalence about the East. Part of his political strength and appeal, one suspects, is that he is a composite of the American dream, or, at least, the middle-class dream, about East and West. In Nixon the two have met, even if they have not necessarily fused psychologically.

# 3

---

# YOUTH
# AND
# MATURITY

★★★★★★★★★★★★★★★★★★★★★★★★★★★★★★★★★★★★★★★★★★★★

**L**ET us return to the young Nixon. What strengths and weaknesses of body and spirit did he bring to his "socialization" process? We are given the picture of a boy prone to illness and physically rather clumsy. We have already noted that Nixon has been susceptible to illnesses of one kind or another since infancy and nearly died of pneumonia when he was four. In addition, he had a severe attack of undulant fever during his senior year at high school and was absent much of that school year. He tended to "motion" sickness; he had hay fever; and he was constantly afraid of getting fat.

Once in college Nixon worked hard to make the football team—unsuccessfully. "A classmate," Mazo and Hess tell us, "recalled that Dick had two left feet. He couldn't coordinate." At meal time he was "too tensed up" to eat.[1] His wife, Pat Nixon, reminiscing about their courtship, remarked that "We liked to do active things like sports of different kinds. We were taking up ice skating, the artificial ice rinks had just opened up and it was the gay thing to do. But it was awful for Dick. He almost broke his head two or three times, but he still kept going."[2]

Nixon seems to have made up in persistence and drive what he lacked in native physical ability. This is an almost classic case of compensation for inferiority, to use the Adlerian notion.[3] Similarly, Nixon also turned his quietness and shyness into extroverted activity, inspiring others by his example. He became an "organizer" and a "doer": he helped form a new fraternity at Whittier College, was elected president of his freshman class, as a junior became chairman of a traditional undergraduate escapade, and so on in the typical pattern of "campus leaders." He seems to have been well liked by everybody. As Pat Nixon

49

recalled, "He was always president of some group . . . so I knew that he would be successful in whatever he undertook."[4]

Nixon's real ability was verbal, if by this we understand not so much an ability to communicate elegantly, but rather an ability to talk one's way through and around topics and situations. He was a debater at Whittier, and this became his primary skill as a politician. Not very good at physical "warfare," he could release his aggressive feelings successfully in oratory. His other strengths were his caution and planning. Lacking spontaneous coordination and the ability to react properly without thought, Nixon turned his weaknesses into strengths. As numerous observers have testified, Nixon "always played it cautious." This trait was combined with the determination to succeed where his father had drifted and failed, and we see the result in the comment of a wartime friend that Nixon "was one guy who knew where he was going. Most of us had big, grandoise schemes. Dick's plans were concise, concrete, and specific."[5]

Thus, the mature Nixon compensated for the physical awkwardness and the propensity to sickness of the young Nixon by careful planning and reliance on verbal and organizing skills.* As he admits on numerous occasions, in times of crisis he experienced all the physical symptoms of tension: edginess, short-temper, inability to eat and to sleep.[6] Are these symptoms especially prominent in Nixon, building on his earlier stresses and strains? Or are they normal to anyone in time of crisis? In any case, as Nixon tells us in *Six Crises,* he learned painstakingly to cope with his tensions and, as he sees it, to use them as a source of strength. The pattern throughout is con-

---

* The physical awkwardness and proneness to sickness still occasionally manifest themselves in the mature Nixon, as when during the 1960 campaign he banged his knee on the door of a car and developed a serious infection that hospitalized him. This incident might be passed over if Nixon had not hurt his knee again on the edge of an automobile door, just as in the first occurrence—but this time as he was entering the television studio for his first debate with Kennedy!

stant: weakness and failure turned into strength and success by dint of sheer persistence and hard work.

The other outstanding trait of the young Nixon was that he was a daydreamer. This sits in rather paradoxical combination with the hard worker; but it is a persistent theme in Nixon's life, probably accounting for much of his reputation as an introspective thinker. He may have become such a doer in order to deny his daydreaming propensity. Young Nixon, we are informed, "preferred daydreams to anything else on earth."[7] "I can still," his aunt, Mrs. Marshburn recalls, "see him lying on the lawn, sky-viewing and daydreaming." Then she continues immediately, "when he was a small boy he wanted his mother to do things for him, and he asked her rather than his father."[8] Were Nixon's daydreams connected on occasion with fantasied gratifications, obtained from his mother? Surely, this would be a normal childhood desire. It is the persistence of daydreaming in Nixon that surprises one.

His constant daydream as a child concerned traveling to far off places. Even more specifically, as we have noted, he dreamed of being "a railroad man." Was this a heightened and successful version of his father's experience as a motorman? Nixon clung to this dream, in spite of his mother's wishes that he become a musician or a preacher, practically until he was in high school. Then, as we have seen, inspired by his father's diatribes against competitive politicians, he decided to become a lawyer-politician.

Still, the dream sequence persisted. Even as a successful politician and Vice President of the United States, Nixon played with a daydream, though this time in terms of a denial:

I suppose this would make a better story if I could fit the facts of my life into the Great American Legend as to how presidential candidates are born and made.

The legend goes something like this. A mother takes a child on her knees. She senses by looking into his eyes that there is something truly extraordinary about him. She says to herself and perhaps even to him, "You, son, are going to be President some day." From that time on, he is tapped for greatness. He talks before he walks. He reads a thousand words a minute. He is bored by school because he is so much smarter than his teachers. He prepares himself for leadership by taking courses in public speaking and political science. He drives ever upward, calculating every step of the way until he reaches his and—less importantly—the nation's destiny by becoming President of the United States.

So goes the legend. The truth in my case is not stranger than fiction perhaps—but it may be more believable.[9]

Nixon's dream, as we have seen, was to be a railroad engineer— "not because of any interest in engines (I have no mechanical aptitude whatever)," he tells us, but because he wanted "to travel and see the United States and the world."[10] When he changed his daydream from railroad man to lawyer-politician— "I will be an old-fashioned kind of lawyer, a lawyer who can't be bought," he had fantasied at age twelve—the "Great American Legend" was the dream he should have had, but did not.

It was, however, the dream that came true for Nixon. There is an extraordinary passage in his acceptance speech to the 1968 Republican Convention, where Nixon links his own dream life to the Great American Dream. Earlier, in the beginning of his campaign he had already talked of "the lift of a driving dream." Now he gave his version of that dream. It is worth quoting the whole passage. First, he talks of all children:

Tonight, I see the face of a child.

He lives in a great city. He is black. He is white. He is Mexican, Italian, Polish. None of this matters. What does matter is that he is an American child.

That child is more important than any politician's promise. He is America. He is a poet, a scientist, a great teacher, a proud craftsman. He is everything we have ever hoped to be and everything we dare to dream to be.

He sleeps the sleep of childhood and dreams its dreams. Yet

when he awakens, he awakens to a living nightmare of poverty, neglect and despair.

He fails in school.

He ends up on welfare.

For him the American system is one that feeds his stomach and starves his soul. It breaks his heart. And in the end it may take his life on some distant battlefield.

To millions of children in this rich land, this is their prospect for the future.[11]

Then Nixon talks of himself.

I see another child.

He hears the train go by at night and dreams of faraway places he would like to go.

It seems like an impossible dream.

But he is helped on his journey through life.

A father who had to go to work before he finished the sixth grade, sacrificed everything so that his sons could go to college.

A gentle, Quaker mother, with a passionate concern for peace, quietly wept when he went to war but understood why he had to go.

A great teacher, a remarkable football coach, an inspirational minister encouraged him on his way.

A courageous wife and loyal children stood by him in victory and defeat.

In his chosen profession of politics, first scores, then hundreds, then thousands, and finally millions worked for his success.

Tonight he stands before you  nominated for President of the United States.

You can see why I believe so deeply in the American Dream.

For most of us the American Revolution has been won; the American Dream has come true.[12]

At the end Nixon exhorts his listeners, "I ask you to help me make that dream come true for millions to whom it is an impossible dream today. This is the cause in which we enlist tonight."[13] There is a dreamlike quality about the whole passage. Nixon had just been made his party's candidate with the support of Southern politicians, such as Senators John Towers and Strom Thurmond, and was about to select Spiro Agnew of Maryland as his Vice President; yet he holds out the American Dream of everyone a potential President to a "black" child, too. He speaks of his Quaker mother, with a passionate concern for *peace,* and then employs the military term "enlist." He talks of the "American Revolution" to a party that dreads revolution of any sort. The sacrificial father, the weeping mother, the land of equal opportunity, they are all there in a dream landscape of America. One can only assume that Nixon's daydreams became a dominant means by which he perceived selected aspects of reality.

Nixon's daydreams are closely connected to his loneliness and his reputation for introspection, as well as to the way in which he makes decisions. Thus, Mrs. Marshburn, after recalling Nixon as the youthful dreamer, added, "In his teens he would sometimes grow weary of the small talk which went on in gatherings, and he would go away by himself to a secluded place, to read or just to be by himself."[14] The general picture is confirmed for us by his brother Donald. "Yes. Dick was always a deep thinker," Donald recollected "Some people thought he was aloof or stuck up because he walked right past them in the street without seeing them. He got totally wrapped up in his thoughts. . . . At family picnics, he would always go off by himself."[15]

Now, we must be careful to place Nixon's "going off by himself" in perspective. This is typical adolescent behavior, described in technical language, by Anna Freud, for example, as "withdrawal." It is a defense during puberty against the over-threatening libidinal attachment to the parents, and an adaptive mechanism for gradually weaning oneself from the shelter of the family, as one reaches out for youthful autonomy. What holds our attention in Nixon's case, therefore, is the persistence and strength of this withdrawal in later life.

Once again, there seems to be a strong identification with his father. As Wills tells us, "Frank Nixon was a loner" in the tight little world of Whittier.[16] Richard Nixon, too, is basically a "loner," making his own way in a hostile world. He likes to be "by himself." In Key Biscayne, we are told, rarely a weekend passes without a solitary swim and a long walk on the beach.[17] His closest frend, Bebe Rebozo, will sit for hours with Nixon, not disturbing him, leaving Nixon "alone."

Nixon's "loner" character corresponds with his brooding, introspective nature. He appears to have been, and for that matter still is, subject to moods of depression. Nixon himself has commented many times that he is an introvert in an extrovert profession, and there is little question that this ambivalent relationship has contributed to the puzzle of the "real" Nixon. Moreover, it is these aspects of his character that have led some people to view him as a "deep thinker," an "intellectual."

What is the significance, the "meaning" of these traits in Nixon? Only an analyst, treating Nixon, could give us a complete explanation. We must be satisfied here with bits and pieces of an answer. Theodore White, who, in fact, abjures psychoanalysis, gives us some interesting hints in his portrait of Nixon in 1960. Nixon, White informs us, has "come to regard the world about him with a wary, forbidding suspicion. A brooding, moody man, given to long stretches of introspection, he trusts only himself and his wife. . . . Richard M. Nixon is a man of major talent—but a man of solitary, uncertain impulse."[18] Suspicion and lack of trust: was Nixon's adolescent world, his mother's presence, even the existence of his brothers and himself so uncertain that only a withdrawal of emotions and isolation could allow him to fend off his fears? While we cannot, alas, be sure of the precise etiology, there can be no doubt as to the general pattern of Nixon's feelings.

Yet for one who wishes to be alone, Nixon has also shown a marked desire for the warmth and approval of crowds. As William P. Rogers, Nixon's Secretary of State, advisor, and one of his closest friends has pointed out, "While he [Nixon] is likely to maintain a serious, almost brooding countenance in the company of three or four persons, he lights up like a Christmas tree when confronted with a crowd. He genuinely loves people."[19] I would suggest that it is not so much that Nixon genuinely loves people as that he wants people genuinely to love him. He is in search of what psychoanalysts call "narcissistic supplies" (as indeed we all are; the question, as always, is one of degree). Such an interpretation would fit with brother Don's recollection of Richard Nixon's intense self-absorption, causing him to walk past people. The same ego involvement can be satisfied by loving oneself, so to speak, or by having amorphous crowds love one.

By 1968, if we can trust one of Nixon's other close friends, Robert Finch, Nixon had come to closer terms with reality and with his own narcissistic needs. "He's still a solitary," Finch remarked. "But he's lost the syndrome of 1960 and 1962. He *doesn't want to be loved;* he's not looking for adulation the way he used to; it's a case of cold respect, he wants respect; that's the lesson that came to him from the 1962 campaign, and if he's come to that point, he offers the potential of being a great leader."[20] We, of course, would say that Nixon, the loner, still wants to be loved. In part he is a loner because he fears that he will *not* be loved; one withdraws from what one cannot have. But while still wanting to be loved, Nixon has learned, as he has in so many areas, how partially to control that need.

The "lonely" quality of Nixon and his introspective nature manifest themselves in the way he makes decisions. "No other candidate of the big seven," White tells us, "operated in 1960 with fewer personnel or kept more of the critical decisions in his own hands."[21] By 1968, however, Nixon had learned that this was largely dysfunctional from a political standpoint. He added staff and dispersed the minor administrative decisions, but the fundamental pattern of lonely major political decisions still held. Nixon constantly surprised his staff by emerging with decisions about which they knew nothing. For example, his decision to name Warren Earl Burger (the play on the name of Earl Warren, Eisenhower's Chief Justice, is striking) to the Supreme Court was shielded from even his closest advisers. And so, on a different political level, was his decision to visit the Lincoln Memorial and talk to the students.

Later, we shall say more about the role of decisions in Nixon's life—how he makes them, and what they mean to him. For the moment we wish only to emphasize the way in which they are related to the lonely, brooding, "introspective" daydreaming quality of Nixon's character. Rooted in his childhood, these qualities have persisted, with subtle modifications, into his adult life and career.

Out of the daydreams came a career choice: to be a lawyer-politician. His father's injunction against crooked politicians rang in his ears. But what, more positively, would a virtuous politician look like? What political ideals would he hold? Nixon himself claims that on the way to becoming a successful lawyer-politician, he started as a "liberal" and ended as a "conservative." Nixon seems to have borrowed his father's admiration for Teddy Roosevelt and Robert LaFollette, his mother's admiration for Woodrow Wilson, and his grandmother's admiration for Abraham Lincoln.[22] There seem to be no political heroes of Nixon's own devising, no turning from the psychological authority of his parents. Like many other students of that period, his public heroes were Justices Brandeis, Cardozo, and Hughes.* As Nixon summed himself up, he was a "liberal" in college, "but not a flaming liberal."

Once in Washington, D.C., however, working for the OPA,

---

\* There is a certain irony in the fact that, determined to defend his nomination of Haynsworth to the Supreme Court, Nixon "spent nights rereading Congressional records of the struggles over the similar controversial nominations of Louis Brandeis and Charles Evans Hughes." (Semple, "Nixon's Presidency Is a Very Private Affair," p. 128).

Nixon apparently experienced a "conversion" (though Nixon's immediate superior recalls that he was "very quiet, self-effacing, conservative,"[23] from the beginning). Nixon's own account is as follows:

I came out of college more liberal than I am today, more liberal in the sense that I thought it was possible for government to do more than I later found it was practical to do. . . . I became more conservative first, after my experience with OPA. . . . I also became greatly disillusioned about bureaucracy and about what the government could do because I saw the terrible paper work that people had to go through. I also saw the mediocrity of so many civil servants. And for the first time when I was in OPA I also saw that there were people in government who were not satisfied merely with interpreting the regulations, enforcing the law that Congress passed, but who actually had a passion to get business and used their government jobs to that end. These were of course some of the remnants of the old, violent New Deal crowd. They set me to thinking a lot at that point.

According to Nixon, in the OPA he learned firsthand how "political appointees at the top feathered their nests with all kinds of overlapping and empire building."[24]

How can we explain what happened? On the most obvious level Nixon had come to identify the "corrupt politicians" of his father's wrath with the "old, violent New Deal crowd." Is there anything more to this episode? Further research will probably help answer this question. At the moment, however, I can only suggest a psychological line of inquiry to use in relation to future information. It emerges from a consideration by a psychologist, Lawrence F. Schiff, of a number of case studies of what he calls "Dynamic Young Fogies—Rebels on the Right." Schiff studies the conversion to conservatism as it occurs at adolescence and sets up two categories: (1) where the conversion occurs immediately following puberty (between twelve and seventeen), and (2) where it takes place in late adolescence (beyond seventeen).

We shall concentrate on this second category. I quote Schiff:

The late converts—whom I call "the obedient rebels"—were the ones most representative of campus conservative activists. Typically they were from homes very much concerned with high status and achievement. In almost all cases their early experiences were dominated by a determined parent, or parents, with detailed and ambitious expectations for their children. All but one were eldest or only sons and the burden of parental ambition fell on them. The obedient rebels (at least in the early years and again after conversion) were usually considered the "good boys" of their families.

Each "rebelled"—sometimes because he felt he could not live up to or realize himself under such pressure—or departed to some degree from the path set out for him. But the revolt was not without peril. Suddenly, he would be horrified to discover (on the campus, in the armed forces, or among the lower-classes) that he was surrounded by "radicalism," "immorality," or personal hardship—something for which his comfortable background had not prepared him. He would reject the new environment totally and become converted to a conservatism not much different from the one he had left in the first place—but which, superficially at least, he had accepted on his own initiative and conviction.

Psychologically, in essence, his conversion was a reaction to the threat of genuine personality changes—which allows great creative possibilities, but also involves dangers. In effect he had come to the pit of change, looked down into it, and turned back, rejecting all alternatives beyond the reaffirmation of obedience.[25]

Did something resembling this pattern happen to Nixon in Washington, D.C.? Do we recognize a familiar note in Schiff's account of one of his case studies: "Herron's conversion took place while he was stationed abroad in the Navy. Disturbed by the 'slothfulness' and 'self-indulgent habits' of the local citizenry, he had a sudden realization of 'the consequences of not subscribing to a strict moral code.' "[26] Is this where any potential "rebellion" against authority became grounded and harmless in the case of Richard Nixon? Only time and future research will answer such questions. All we can now say with certainty is that Nixon experienced some sort of significant reassertion of conservative beliefs while in the big city of Washington, D.C.*

For Nixon that reassertion of conservative beliefs, sparked by his OPA experience and the revelation of the iniquities of big government, was to persist throughout the rest of his career, and to find a major correspondence in his political situation. It fitted perfectly, for example, with his own infatuation with foreign policy—far places?—and comparative disinterest in domestic affairs. "I've always thought this country could run itself domestically," he said in 1968, "without a President; all you need is a competent Cabinet to run the country at home. You need a President for foreign policy; no Secretary of State is really important; the President makes foreign policy."[27] In short, Nixon's belief in the least government possible corresponded perfectly with his dislike of domestic concerns.

So, too, it fitted into his Southern Strategy of that same year. In his State of the Union message, Nixon reiterated his faith in "local government," which had been and must be "closest" and "most responsive to the people." Local government necessarily was "far more intimate" with the citizenry than any

* As this book was being prepared for press, an article by Milton Viorst on Nixon's OPA experience appeared that provides further confirmation of my hunches, especially along the lines of the Schiff analysis. ("Nixon of the O.P.A.," *New York Times Magazine,* October 3, 1971.) Viorst tells us how Nixon's immediate superior at OPA, Thomas E. Harris, "always felt Nixon was uncomfortable among the liberals, the Eastern law-school graduates, the Jews he rubbed shoulders with on the job. No one thought of him as a right-winger in those days, Harris said, but in style if not in politics he was thought of as conservative. Because he lacked sophistication and the big-city graces, he never quite fit in." Viorst himself concludes that "it is clear that Nixon emerged from the O.P.A. not only with a strong distaste for the agency but with a bitterness toward the people who had surrounded him in his work. 'The short time I spent in the O.P.A. was a good education for me,' he told an interviewer in the nineteen-fifties. 'I saw later in my political career the same type of people angling for something and anxious not to miss the bandwagon.'"

"bureaucratic elite in Washington." The time was at hand for "power" to be removed from the national capital and "turned back to the people." Fueled by Nixon's strong personal feelings, going back to his OPA days, such "conservative" sentiments took on new meaning in a time of civil rights agitations. "Power to the people" meant one thing for Nixon and his Southern supporters; another thing for black people across the nation.

Exactly how important, and even traumatic, that earliest experience in the OPA was for Nixon can be seen in its persisting role in his economic policy, first in his adamant opposition to wage and price controls and, then, after his reversal on this issue, his continued reluctance to acknowledge the need for bureaucratic enforcement machinery. While almost all observers, and even Nixon's own chairman of the Council of Economic Advisors, Paul McCracken, agreed in 1969 that wage and price controls were necessary to combat the continuing inflation raising havoc with the American economy—and, incidentally, eroding Nixon's chances for re-election—Nixon refused to go along. When presented at that time with the wage and price control suggestion, Nixon burst out, "Controls. Oh my God, no! I was a lawyer for the OPA during the war and I know all about controls. They mean rationing, black markets, inequitable administration. We'll never go for controls."[28] Merely noting here the interesting fact that the highly "controlled" Nixon is fanatically against government controls, we must conclude that in this instance ideological stance is deeply rooted in Nixon's personal experience in the OPA, as he moved from being a "liberal" to a "conservative." (Later, we shall examine in some detail his about-face on the wage-price issue in the light of all that we have said here.)

As we have seen, by the time of college and law school, Nixon had made a career choice and had developed many of his political and ideological positions. At this time he also faced a choice as to the woman who would accompany him on his career. We are used to anthropologists studying the courtship patterns of small societies; surely, with even more justification, psychologists ought to study the courtship pattern of individuals. Above all, a man's marriage tells us much about who he is, as well as helping to shape what he will be in the future. Therefore, Richard Nixon's courtship and marriage to Pat Ryan reveal more than might appear at first glance.

Before he met his future wife, we are told, Nixon had neither time nor money to be a ladies' man. Nevertheless, according to Mazo and Hess, "He dated the daughter of the local police chief steadily before going east to law school."[29] Some of that lady's reminiscences have recently appeared, and they provide us with some rich insights.[30] Ola-Florence Welch (now Mrs. Jobe) and Richard Nixon, we are told, went together almost six years; one year in high school, four years in college, and one when Nixon was at Duke Law School. Most of their friends expected them to get married. There is no doubt that it was a serious romance.

The two met in a Whittier High School play, *Aeneas and Dido,* where each had a leading role. "Dick was a marvelous actor," Ola-Florence remembers, "quick, perceptive, responsive, industrious. He was industrious in everything. Persistent. Bulldog terrier. And he always had great stage presence and an almost instinctive rapport with his audience. I honestly believe that if he had made the stage his career instead of studying law—he majored in history—I'm sure he would have developed into a top-notch leading man."[31] Surprisingly, to those who see Nixon as a jowlly stiff figure on television, Ola-Florence remembers him as "really quite handsome. He was tall and good-looking." Then, in a rather warm and winning fashion, she admits that sex appeal may have played its part. "I don't know why in retrospect I found Richard Nixon so fascinating and interesting. I am not counting out sex appeal, which as a subject, believe me, we didn't discuss in those days." The other, probably deepest attraction, however, lay in Nixon's mental qualities. "You have no idea," Ola-Florence stresses, "how tremendously interesting and engrossing he was to me, the daughter of a small-town police chief. I considered myself provincial and him worldly." She explains as the continuing attraction, "most of all it was because of his mind. He had a fine mind."

Thus, Nixon's industrious mental qualities had helped to gain him the favors of Ola-Florence. What was her attraction for him? From her school pictures, we can see that one part of the answer is simply that she was a very attractive girl. Good humor, warmth, and fun are written all over her face. Her admiration for Nixon's mental qualities—the traits that lifted him out of the small town mold—must have appealed to his *amour propre*. And, lastly, constant arguing seems to have added to the zest of the romance. Ola-Florence came from a strong Democratic family, just as Nixon came from a strong Republican family. "I guess that's why Dick and I used to argue so much," Ola-Florence reminisced, "we had marvelous talks."

It is not a particularly unusual picture of a certain sort of adolescent love relation, although the fact that it lasted six years is unusual. Why did it break up? Another classmate at Whittier offers an explanation. "He [Nixon] was combative," this source recalls, "rather than conciliatory. He had a nasty temper. He seemed to me to lack tenderness and warmth. I remember one time he took Ola-Florence to a dance, a prom. She was fun-loving and gay although she was basically shy around boys, because there were only sisters in her family. But she was stubborn. So, too, was Richard. They got into a quarrel, and he simply walked out on her. She had to phone her folks to come fetch her."

The very qualities that helped bring them together—mental

attraction and frequent arguments—also served to pull them apart. The final dramatic breakup, however, came in fairly typical adolescent fashion. The same classmate tells us that:

My own recollection is that in our senior year when Ola-Florence took for granted that she was Richard's girl and he was her beau, he took another girl out. She then asked Gail Jobe of Corvina to some function, and Gail wound up taking her to the senior prom. Richard got uptight about it, and he ended up taking somebody else—I think Marjorie Hildreth—to the senior prom. I think that was the opening wedge in their breakup. But even after that, they seemed to have patched things up and were going together.

I remember another time—this was after graduation and Richard was away at Duke Law School. He came home and phoned Ola-Florence for a date. Well, she was dating Gail Jobe and still keeping Richard on the string, I guess. Anyway, Richard phoned and said, "Ola, I'm coming over." The poor girl—she had Gail in her living room at the time—so what could she say but no?

Richard was furious. With that temper of his, he went through the roof. "Don't worry," he stormed, "you'll never hear from me again."

Spurned and spurning, the situation, though typical, is not entirely clear. Nixon's temper was obviously a factor. In any case, even after this last episode just mentioned, Nixon continued to write Ola-Florence from Duke Law School, at least once a week, but the romance was over. "His letters," Ola-Florence recalls, "were well-written and informative. Nothing mushy. He always kept himself in check." Nixon, it would appear, had had his one possibly fatal attraction to someone almost the direct opposite of himself—the other identity. But something inside made it necessary, it seems, for him to reject this side; to "keep himself in check." Ola-Florence, I think, best perceived what was involved. "I knew," she remarked, "that Dick would amount to something, but never in my wildest dreams did I ever picture him then as President of the United States. I'm sure he would not have made it if I had married him. I loved fun too much. I'm convinced the girl he chose was the perfect mate for him. Certainly, she's proven that."

The six-year romance with Ola-Florence could not help being of great significance in Nixon's emotional life. It was a crucial part of his self-development and self-definition; an immensely important part of his "testing" period. The way was now open for his meeting with his future wife, whom he met two years after Ola-Florence married Gail Jobe. Meanwhile, at Duke, we are told, "he attended occasional dances as a stag."[32] Once back in Whittier, as a struggling lawyer, he attended a tryout for a Little Theater play. There he met Catherine Patricia Thelma Ryan, a new schoolteacher of commercial subjects.

Pat Ryan, who, according to Mazo and Hess, was two months younger than Nixon, but according to other sources was actually over a year older, was born in Ely, Nevada. She was the daughter of a miner who moved his family to California (about eighteen miles from Los Angeles) and had taken up farming. Everyone in the family worked together, and the picture we have of their life then is a very pleasant one. When Pat was twelve, her mother died, and the young girl took on the responsibility for the house. Her father died five years later. Graduating from high school, Pat worked in the local bank for a year, went East with relatives for a year or so (working during that time in a hospital near New York), and returned to Los Angeles to attend the University of Southern California. To earn money she took on bit parts in movies, though her real love was merchandising. The opportunity of making more money in a teaching job unexpectedly caused her to shift vocation and come to Whittier. A friend trying out for a Little Theatre play persuaded her to come along, where her "fated" meeting with Richard Nixon occurred. We need only note that Nixon met both of the important women in his love life through dramatics.

That very night Nixon proposed. Mazo and Hess report Pat as saying, "I thought he was nuts or something. I guess I just looked at him. I couldn't imagine anyone ever saying anything like that so suddenly. Now that I know Dick much better I can't imagine that he would ever say that, because he is very much the opposite, he's more reserved."[33] Though she admired Nixon from the beginning, she was in no mood to settle down; she had visions of travel, she tells us. (Had he not explained his dream of travel to her?) But Richard Nixon persisted. (As we have already seen, he was prepared to break his neck ice skating. Although earlier talked into taking dancing lessons by Ola-Florence, Nixon, still not very accomplished, kept trying.) While Pat kept on dating, Nixon gave up all other dates (no real sacrifice on his part). Mazo and Hess give us the extraordinary information that "he hung around dutifully even when she had other dates and would drive her to Los Angeles if she was to meet someone there, and wait around to take her home."[34] Finally, in the spring of 1940 Pat said yes and they were married on June 21, 1940.*

What is the significance and meaning of Nixon's courtship? The first thing to notice is his unusual impulsive behavior: proposing to Pat Ryan on their first meeting. At first it seems, as it did later to Pat, "out of character." I suspect that it was not, and that it just appears impulsive and out of character. Given the general pattern of Nixon's behavior—cautious, planned, and contrived—we are on better ground postulating his proposal to Pat not as an impulsive exception, but as part of a "plan," though perhaps an unconscious one, concerning the

---

* Garry Wills allows us to make an interesting analogy to Nixon's dating behavior. Discussing the various "dump Nixon" episodes over the years, he remarks on "That gaucheness of a man lingering on when he is no longer wanted [which] becomes, at a certain point, the crazy proof of his importance. He survived. He was often a leftover, but he always found some job to perform in that capacity." (Wills, *Nixon Agonistes,* p. 6.)

girl he wished to marry. We have already remarked on his propensity to daydream. I suspect plan and dream came together in the person of Pat Ryan, and Nixon acted accordingly, with complete deliberation. Persistence did the rest.

There is another possible explanation. If we could be sure about his parents' marriage, we could speculate about possible overdetermination. (See p. 159ff. for a discussion of overdetermination.) According to one biographer, William Costello, Frank Nixon met Hannah Milhous on February 15, 1908, and four months and ten days later they were married.[35] Another biographer, Bela Kornitzer, however, tells us that two years elapsed from the time Frank Nixon met Hannah to their marriage.[36] How convenient if Costello were right, and Richard Nixon had his father's example before him (how quickly had he proposed?) to emulate in an "impulsive" marriage. Alas, a recalcitrant "fact" and a highly speculative psychological inference do not make for very secure psychohistory.

The second thing to notice about his conquest of Pat Ryan is that it was his first real success. At about the time he met Pat, Nixon had helped set up the Citra-Frost Co. to market frozen orange juice, a venture that, apparently through no fault of his, folded after a year and a half. Earlier he had failed to secure a job in an Eastern law firm. Failure to win Pat Ryan would have been a tremendous blow coming on top of the others; success undoubtedly gave him a great uplift. As Freud has remarked (and I paraphrase), "To win the girl of one's dreams is to have the feeling that all of nature is on one's side."

Moreover, and this is the third point to notice, Pat Nixon undoubtedly brought Nixon real strength; in the pattern of his own parents she seemed, in fact, the stronger of the two. Loyally, she stood by him through failure and success; patiently, she worked in his campaigns. There is some evidence that she would have preferred some other life than the political —the attack on the Nixons, culminating in the "Checkers

Speech" of 1952, especially, seems to have soured her, and she even prevailed upon Nixon to write out a decision to retire from politics after his term as Vice President ended in 1957 and to put this note in his wallet—but always she followed where he led. Yet even Nixon admitted that she was the more decisive and stronger of the two. In the 1952 Fund controversy it was Pat who insisted that Nixon could not resign under fire. Three minutes before he was to make his famous talk, Nixon tells us, he turned to Pat and said, " 'I just don't think I can go through with this one.' 'Of course you can,' she said, with the firmness and confidence in her voice that I so desperately needed."[37] During his speech Pat was present in the studio, within camera range, visible to Nixon. In the campaign of 1960, Nixon informs us, "Her physical stamina had been even greater than mine. In the long hand-shaking sessions, it was I, rather than she, who would first have to ask for a break in the line."[38] In Caracas and in Moscow Pat Nixon showed similar sang-froid and decisiveness. Thus, in marrying Pat, Nixon gained great strength, both in successfully winning her, and in the affirmation of his own possibilities for success that lay in her acquiescence in his persistence and determination.

True, as in all his relations, Richard Nixon may have had to pay a price for this accession to strength. Some observers seem to see Pat as not sufficiently supportive of Nixon, perhaps even undercutting and humiliating him in public. One of Nixon's early political advisers, Father John Cronin (who helped Nixon as a sort of brain trust in his anticommunist studies), said, "I don't think that Pat helped him. In the nineteen sixty-five campaign, Dick prepared the last draft of a speech on a tape recorder, but some aide had not fixed the recorder properly, so nothing was on the tape. After all that work, he had to deliver an earlier draft—mine. His heart was not in it, so he gave it a poor delivery. And Pat chewed the hell out of him in front of the staff."[39] Earl Mazo makes a similar point in his revelation that when Nixon, who had put in writing his agreement to give up politics, told her at a dinner party that he was going to run for governor of California, she "chewed him out" in public.

Unlike Father Cronin, I find myself unsure as to who is at fault here, and I feel a good deal of sympathy for Pat Nixon. After all, it was the husband who was first betraying the wife, not vice versa. Nevertheless, it is possible that Pat can be viewed as undercutting her husband in various ways. Moreover, at some level Pat's very strength may touch on some masochistic need of Nixon's to confront again his own self-doubt and fear of weakness. Garry Wills makes an interesting though awkward comment on Frank Nixon's marriage. "His moderate success at feeding his family during the Depression was poisoned by the fact that his wife—a college graduate (Whittier, 1906) though he did not finish grade school, a local saint people flocked to (carefully steering around him)— was the presiding personality of the store, accounting for its popularity. It is hard to be married to a saint, even a real one."[40] Richard Nixon had no need to feel socially or educationally inferior to Pat; but one does sense elements of a repetition of his father's life in being married to a "saint" (for a number of sources suggest this is how Pat appears to many people).

But granting this possibility—another source of Nixon's ambivalences—I would nonetheless reaffirm the more important fact that Pat has given Nixon great strength. As everyone attests, Nixon's mother, Hannah, was a very "strong woman," who was also sensitive. Speaking in 1971 of his wife, who was about to celebrate her fifty-ninth birthday, Nixon similarly described her as a woman "of great strength of character"—a "sundowner," that is, a strict disciplinarian—of "superb sensitivity." Returning often to the thesis, as the interview puts it, "that a President needs a woman of character and strength behind him," Nixon commented that Pat "is in that tradition." "The wife," he added, "has to be the stronger partner of the two."[41]

Nixon had dated Ola-Florence, who liked fun, for six years; he married Pat, who, like his mother, was a woman of great strength. This in itself was a major accession to Nixon's political career. Moreover, insofar as Pat embodied some of his mother's qualities (and we assume a certain amount of transference here, as in all such relations), her accepting him also meant approval and acceptance of his decision to enter the "warfare of politics," in spite of her later wavering and unhappiness over that very decision.

Before we leave the years of Nixon's youth and young manhood when his character was formed and consider his political patterns of behavior and beliefs, we need to look briefly at another element in his make-up: acting. Nixon's career as an actor blossomed at Whittier College. We are told that he collaborated in writing his fraternity's first play, a "shocker," entitled *The Trysting Place,* and was its director and male lead. We have seen that he met Ola-Florence at a high school play, and Pat Ryan at a Little Theatre tryout. Such facts make us look twice at the picture of Nixon as a shy, introspective boy.

On seeing Nixon weeping on Senator Knowland's shoulder after the Checkers Speech, one of his Whittier teachers made an interesting comment on his acting ability. "I taught him how to cry," Dr. Upton remembered, "in a play by John Drinkwater called *Bird in Hand.* He tried conscientiously at rehearsals, and he'd get a pretty good lump in his throat and that was all. But on the evenings of performance tears just ran right out of his eyes. It was beautifully done, those tears"[42]*

---

* In another account Dr. Upton reportedly added, "But it was a sincere performance, and there is nothing perfidious or immoral about being a good actor" (Kornitzer, *The Real Nixon,* p. 107); however, this addition does not undercut the point I am making.

Nixon obviously learned his lesson well and in later life rose to the occasions. For a "strong" man it is strange how often he breaks down in tears. We are told that on the evening of his Checkers Speech, "when a 'Have Faith' message was handed him from his mother, Nixon stepped into a vacant room to hide his tears."[43] After the speech itself—one of the most sentimental political speeches in all of American history, embarrassing even to many of Nixon's partisans—"when he reached the dressing room, Nixon turned away from his friends and let loose the tears he had been holding back."[44] When Eisenhower put his arm around Nixon, "Nixon turned his head to the window and tried to keep back the tears."[45] Nixon explained these effusions by saying that he cried because he had exhausted all his "emotional reserve."[46] In his introduction to *Six Crises* he claims, "I have found leaders are subject to all the human frailties. . . . Sometimes even strong men will cry."[47]*

Nixon is right in his analysis of leaders. But the words of Dr. Upton, "It was beautifully done, those tears," cast a strange light on Nixon's Rousseau-like performances. Certainly, Nixon himself felt he was an authority on when other people were acting, and this "intuition" on his part seems to play an im-

---

* It is interesting to note that Nixon's foreign policy advisor, Henry A. Kissinger, in his psychological study of Bismarck, points out that "the apostle of the claims of power was subject to fits of weeping in a crisis." ("The White Revolutionary: Reflections on Bismarck," *Daedalus* 98 [1968]: 890.) This article opens up fascinating speculations about the comparisons and "transferences" Kissinger may be making between Bismarck and Nixon; for example, compare also the observation that "it was not that Bismarck lied—this is much too self-conscious an act—but that he was finely attuned to the subtlest currents of any environment and produced measures precisely adjusted to the need to prevail. The key to Bismarck's success was that he was always sincere." (Ibid., p. 898.) (In all fairness I ought to indicate that some of my "transferences," though in a different context, may be spotted in my own article, "James Mill and the Utilitarians," ibid., pp. 1036–1061.) Aside from "transferences," a close reading of Kissinger's article can shed light on some of his, and therefore perhaps President Nixon's, fundamental foreign policy attitudes.

portant role in much of his political activity. We have already noted Ola-Florence's comment on his "almost instinctive rapport with his audience." Similarly, he frequently talked about the Hiss case as if it were a sort of stage play, a momentous soap opera. The stage itself was set for the Hiss-Chambers confrontation at the Commodore Hotel in New York. Nixon even remembers the "decor": "The living room was decorated with Audubon prints." and, he concludes, "We then proceeded to set up the room."[48]

The "actors" play out their roles. In an earlier interview Nixon tells how he became convinced that Chambers was telling the truth: "His [Chambers'] voice broke and there was a pause of at least 15 to 20 seconds during which he attempted to gain control of his emotions before he could proceed. This one incident was to have a considerable bearing upon my own attitude toward him because I did not feel that it was an *act*. . . . On the contrary, I felt he indicated deep sincerity and honesty."[49] Hiss, on the contrary, comes through as a ham actor: "I felt he had *put on a show* when he was shown a picture of Chambers . . . his statement 'This might look like you, Mr. Chairman,' seemed to me to be *overacted . . .*"[50] According to Nixon, this hearing "showed the committee the *real* Hiss because, except for a few minutes at the beginning and . . . end . . . he *acted* the part of a liar who had been caught, rather than the part of the outraged innocent man, which he had so successfully portrayed before then."[51]

Nixon's own "performances" were obviously far more professional. After his emotional Checkers Speech, he received a phone call from Darryl Zanuck, the Hollywood producer. "The most tremendous performance I've ever seen," was the comment of this professional.[52] Now one does not have to equate Nixon with Hiss—I, for one, have no doubt that Nixon was "clear" of the corruption charges leveled against him, while the evidence against Hiss is quite strong—to realize that Nixon's training in acting must have stood him in good stead during his performance. Nixon seemed to have sensed this himself, when he remarked in disgust about the televised Army-McCarthy hearings: "I prefer professionals to amateur actors."[53]

Even in the international arena, with foreign-speaking politicians, Nixon felt he could distinguish between acting and sincerity. Speaking of Khrushchev's reaction to the Captive Nations Resolution, asking for prayer for the liberating of "enslaved people," passed by Congress just before Nixon's trip, he says, "I was sure that he was going through an *act*—that he was using the resolution as a pretext for taking the offensive against me. . . ."[54] Nixon also told of speaking to Zhukov about the behavior of the Soviet police and crowds: " 'Mr. Zhukov,' I said, 'this little game you've been playing with me through your planted hecklers for the past few days has not been going well with the press, and in my opinion it is backfiring even among your own people. You underestimate their intelligence. They aren't dumb. They know when somebody is acting and when it's the real thing—particularly when the acts have been so amateurish.' "[55]

Nixon, then, was constantly concerned with acting. At one point he informs us that during the 1960 campaign his problem was to hold the Republican vote (the minority party) and then persuade five to six million Democrats to leave their own candidate and vote Republican. "I recognized that I could accomplish this only as President Eisenhower had—by *acting* [Nixon means this in the sense of "action," but the other meaning inheres in it] and speaking not just as a Republican partisan but as a representative of all the people. My trips to Caracas and Moscow had provided an opportunity for me to appear in this *role*."[56] Nixon's highest praise for Pat's campaigning is that she was "a good trouper."[57] So, too, Nixon remarked in a 1966 interview that "occasionally I say a good word for Johnson or Humphrey. *It's a device, of course, to show I'm fair-minded. . . .*"[58]

Of course, all American politicians must play many "roles"

and "act" many parts. Moreover, Nixon's own Thespian experiences may have given him greater empathy for the "acts" of the Hisses and Khrushchevs whom he encountered on the political stage. However, Nixon's empathy may also carry a good deal of projection with it. We can be sure that Nixon's attitude to acting is more significant and more conscious than that of most politicians. The suspicion arises that the "real" Richard Nixon may have been lost in the variety of "roles" in which he has acted. As with other professional actors, the man becomes his roles—and that is his character.

But, having said all that, one must quickly add that Nixon's acting probably serves extremely important political functions. A leader must communicate effectively with his followers: Nixon obviously "reaches" through the new medium of television a large segment of the American population, especially the middle class. His ability to play a role lends itself to the pragmatic politics so typical of America; Nixon, unlike Sir Thomas More, is a "man for all seasons." Whatever ideological commitments inhere in Nixon's personality development, they are severely tempered by his devotion to "acting."

Let us look a bit more closely at Nixon's role-playing, for this is a critical aspect of Nixon's character. Nixon generally speaks of being a railroad engineer or a lawyer, rather than of driving a locomotive or pleading a case. It is the *role,* not the *activity,* that is foremost in his mind. Moreover, the particular roles that he finally emphasized—actor, lawyer, politician—have as their basic content the *necessity* of taking on a role and playing a part: any part. All of these roles fitted in with Nixon's need to argue, and, as we have already noted, to argue on either side of an issue.

To go further, it is my thesis that on the deepest level role serves overdetermined functions in Nixon's psychic economy. Role, in fact, substitutes for an insecurely held self. If one is not sure of what one is, one can at least be one's role. The role then tells us what to do and how to act. To a Nixon filled with "self-doubt," role has a powerful affirmative quality. Garry Wills suggests that Nixon is a "marketable" personality, that is, "there is one Nixon only, though there seem to be new ones all the time—he will try to be what people want."[59] Whatever truth there is to this view—and surely all American politicians fall partly under this description—I am suggesting that in Nixon's case the matter lies deeper.

For Nixon having a role facilitates and possibly even allows him to make decisions (otherwise, as we shall see, a difficult matter). Indeed, it is the role that makes one's decision and that determines one's character. As a lawyer in New York, it is the "fast track" that requires one to keep running and competing, not one's own desires. The role also allows one to act out one's aggressions; thus, it is not I, Nixon, who wishes to get Hiss or thump Khrushchev; it is my duty as a congressman or Vice President. Without a role one is directionless, inhibited in release of aggression, unsure of self. In this connection, too, I suspect that part of Nixon's constant introspection stems in part from his sense of an insecurely held self; he is insistently examining himself to find out who he really is. Fortunately, the role supplies the answer.

In the 1968 campaign Nixon's political advisers unwittingly made the most of this aspect of Nixon's character. They arranged for a series of "spontaneous" questioners in the little town of Hillsboro, New Hampshire, taped the show, and then mechanically edited it. As Theodore White summarizes the proceedings, "Nixon had been 'grouchy' when first pressed into the new form. But with newsmen banned from the sessions, he began to relax, to enjoy the procedure, and, finally, would not stop. With the Hillsboro tapes, cut and chipped into five-minute segments, the media directors of the Nixon effort had their answer; he was crisp, direct, real and convincing. They could present snatches of Nixon, packaged but genuine, wherever they wanted both in New Hampshire and across the nation."[60] "Snatches of Nixon" in his various roles:

Nixon as decisive, sincere, fair-minded, and so forth. In each role Nixon would be comfortable, acting with great stage presence. It is the synthesis, or lack of it, of the roles in the total personality that makes his audience uncomfortable, and leads to disturbing speculation about who is the "real" Nixon.

Once elected President, Nixon has swung into his role with great relish; he obviously *enjoys* his new role. Earlier, he had inflated minor crises (as in *Six Crises*) into events of cosmic importance; this was also a means of inflating his sense of self. Now the inflation and the reality come closer together in actuality. One notices, too, Nixon's increasing use of "I": "I" do this, "I" order that. White perceptively noted that: "Nixon's speech, previously, had always been marked by a somewhat self-deprecating use of the word 'I,' the politician's use of the pronoun as of a detached and distinct *dramatis personae*. Now, in discussing the Cabinet, the word 'I' was used flatly, not as an overbearing man would use it, nor as a pompous man would use it, but as if forty-eight hours in the Presidency had stripped the pronoun bare. 'I ran the meeting,' he said. 'I believe I should run the meetings—all Cabinet meetings. A meeting means more if the President runs it, and I find my attention will stray unless I do run a meeting.' "[61] Since White wrote, Nixon's use of the "I" has become even more frequent (and a little more pompous). "I" is the President. As President, Nixon's role requires him to be, or to appear, decisive and the "I" verbal form underlines this decisiveness. In the office of President, Nixon believes that his role and his self have finally come together. Others may simply see him in his greatest "role."

A word must now be said of a close cousin of Nixon's role-playing and acting abilities: his skill as a debater. As with his acting experience, this, too, seems to have flowered in college. It first became politically important for Nixon in his 1946 Congressional campaign against the incumbent Jerry Voorhis. The two men had five debates, and, according to Mazo and

Hess, Nixon believes "the turning point for him, as the under-dog, was the first debate. 'It was tough,' Nixon says. 'I was the challenger, and he was the experienced incumbent. Once that debate was over, I was on my way to eventual victory.' "[62]

In the light of this debate, we must look at his more famous debates with John F. Kennedy in the 1960 election. Why did Nixon, then in Voorhis' position as an "incumbent," agree to debate the relatively unknown Kennedy? "He [Nixon] had no reason to help build up an audience for Kennedy," Theodore Sorenson wrote. The explanation Nixon gave—that the other people wanted the debates—is weak. Mazo and Hess grasp the truth when they write:

But there seems to us to be another, perhaps overpowering reason why Nixon chose to debate, namely, *he was convinced he could win.* Nixon's whole career had led him to this conclusion—he had been elected to Congress by outdebating his opponent in 1946; he had stayed on the ticket in 1952 by his effective use of television; he reached his highest popularity after the "Kitchen Debate" with Khruschchev in 1959. Now by combining debating and television he could impress millions of Democrats and independents (who he could not otherwise reach) and put the election on ice.[63]

Clearly, Nixon believed intensely in his own verbal skills. He had built much of his political career on them. How could he consider for a moment that he would "lose" to Kennedy when he was choosing the weapons.*

Another reason is that Nixon constantly has to test himself in order to quiet his self-doubts and his continuous fear of failure. In *Six Crises* he offers us his reason for accepting the Kennedy debates. "Had I refused the challenge," he writes, "I would

---

* Theodore White suggests that the very weapon of debate was faulty and ill suited the television media. "For Mr. Nixon was debating with Mr. Kennedy as if a board of judges were scoring points; he rebutted and refuted, as he went, the inconsistencies or errors of his opponent. Nixon was addressing himself to Kennedy—but Kennedy was addressing himself to the audience that was the nation." (White, *Making of President, 1960,* p. 326.)

have opened myself to the charge that I was *afraid* to defend the Administration's and my own record."[64] Theodore White catches much of what was involved in the debates for Nixon when he writes, "he [Nixon] was concerned with the cool and undisturbed man who sat across the platform from him, with the personal adversary in the studio, not with the mind of America."[65] In accusing Kennedy of "running America down and giving us an inferiority complex," in insisting that "there is no reason for a second-rate psychology on the part of any American,"[66] Nixon seemed to be defending himself as much as he was his country.

In this same connection it is interesting to note that in his unnecessary and disastrous press conference after his 1962 gubernatorial defeat, Nixon placed his relations with the press on an agonistic basis, telling reporters that "you've had an opportunity to attack me and I think I've given as good as I've taken. I have welcomed the opportunity *to test wits with you*."[67] Thus, in formal debate, such as with Kennedy, as well as in informal encounters with reporters Nixon could give way to his aggressive impulses at the same time as he tested himself. Making full use of his verbal and acting skills in debate provided a wonderful release, with an extremely high chance of a successful outcome. It is no wonder that Nixon fancied himself as a debater and a performer.

Infancy—Richard Nixon, aged three, with his mother Hannah, his brother Donald on his mother's lap, his father Francis; and his brother Harold. (UPI photo)

Boyhood—Nixon, aged twelve, with his three brothers: Donald (in tire) and, from left to right, Richard, Harold (wearing cap), and Arthur. The childhood deaths of Harold and Arthur had a profound effect on the psychological development of the young Nixon (see p. 22). (Pictorial Parade photo)

Nixon as he grew from boyhood to young manhood. From left: at age 4; playing the violin in the Fullerton, California high school orchestra; at age 18; as a freshman at Duke Law School; and as a lieutenant commander in the U.S. Navy during World War II. (Wide World photos)

The football player—Richard Nixon at Whittier College. Football has always had a deep symbolic significance for Richard Nixon. (UPI photo)

An old friend—President Nixon chatting with Mrs. Gail Jobe (center), the former Ola Florence Welch, whom he had dated as a young man for a period of six years prior to his meeting with Pat Ryan, the future Mrs. Nixon (see p. 62). The occasion was a White House reception for members of his graduating class at Whittier College. (UPI photo)

A group picture—President Nixon and the First Lady pose with members of Nixon's graduating class. (UPI photo)

Thelma (Pat) Ryan, Nixon's future wife. This picture is taken from her high school yearbook.

Early years in Washington—With Pat Nixon and baby Tricia. Nixon, then (1947) a freshman Congressman from California, on a family outing under Washington's cherry blossoms. (UPI photo)

The Hiss Affair—Nixon's role in the Hiss Affair first cast him into the national spotlight. His handling of the case had profound psychological meanings for him also (see p. 90).

A

B

The Checkers Affair (1952)—The most traumatic of Nixon's "six crises."

A. The famous Checkers Speech, when, deserted by most of his party, Nixon, in a nationwide telecast successfully defended his acceptance of an $18,000 political defense fund. (Wide World photo)

B. Nixon breaks down—A rare photo of Nixon crying. He had just learned that President Eisenhower had finally come out in his defense after listening to the favorable response to Nixon's Checkers Speech. (Wide World photo)

C. "He's my boy" again—Nixon stands with Eisenhower on platform during rally at Wheeling, West Virginia. (Wide World photo)

C

The Kitchen Debate—With Soviet Premier Khrus
chev in front of display kitchen area at the U.
Exhibit in Moscow. A skilled debater ever since h
college days at Whittier, Nixon's reliance on h
verbal skills has enabled him to "release his a
gressive feelings through oratory"—making him
formidable political opponent (see p. 123).
(Wide World photo)

Running for the Presidency—This time successful
   On foot. (UPI photo)
   On the TV screen. (Wide World photo)

residential poses and controversial themes.

With Vice President Agnew. (UPI photo)

With his friend Bebe Rebozo (foreground right) and TV producer Paul Keyes. What can we learn from the kind of men Nixon chooses to work and play with (see p. 119)? (Wide World photo)

With some shipbuilders as a "hard hat." (Wide World photo)

The Presidential Nixon—Posing for pictures prior to delivering a television address on the Vietnam war. (Wide World photo)

# 4

---

# PERSONAL CRISES IN A POLITICAL SETTING

★★★★★★★★★★★★★★★★★★★★★★★★★★★★★★★★★★★★★★★★★★★

**W**HAT was the content of Nixon's political debates? His reputation was based on his "anticommunist" positions, and these need now to be examined. We must start with a paradox: Though as a congressman Nixon came from an isolationist district, he quickly showed himself an internationalist in orientation. Thus, he worked on the Herter Committee, whose report led to the Marshall Plan, and considered this the most important service of his congressional career. From the very beginning of his political life, Nixon showed his inclination toward the Eastern Establishment and its internationalist position.

But Nixon gave internationalism a very special twist by combining it with a Western fundamentalist attack on communism. By vehemently attacking communism, Nixon was defending Americanism. Indeed, one could then define the latter by the former action, allowing oneself the luxury of polarizing feelings, so that total hate could flow out to the enemy and total love to one's "own" people. Yet, as we shall see at the end, there is a certain strange identification with the "enemy," the "Devil," which must be strenuously denied.

We must always keep in mind, however, the context in which Nixon operated. The late 1940s saw the beginning of the cold war. Although domestic communism was not as strong an issue in the 1948 election as it was to become a few years later with Joseph McCarthy, it was now linked, by Nixon and others, with the sensitive theme of corruption. In the Fund controversy, for example, Nixon defended himself by saying, "I was warned that if I continued to attack the Communists and crooks in this [Truman's] Government, they would continue to smear me."[1] After 1948, threats of recession, the outbreak of the Korean War, and all the other Soviet-American developments supplied the background of fear in which anti-communism flourished. Nixon was merely a "typical" American in much of his position.

Nixon's anticommunism first publicly manifested itself in his debates with Congressman Voorhis, whom he attacked as a frontman for the "Communist-dominated PAC" and suggested that he was one of those "lip-service Americans . . . who front for un-American elements, wittingly, or otherwise, by advocating increasing federal controls over the lives of the people."[2] (Here, incidentally, we see a trace of Nixon's OPA "conversion" experience, now linked to anticommunism.) In opposition to Voorhis' "un-Americanism," Nixon resorted to the sentimental promise "to preserve our sacred heritage in the name of my buddies and your loved ones, who died that these might endure." Some critics, however, have wondered whether Nixon believed his own statement following his victory: "Our campaign was a very honest debate on the issues."[3]

In any case the pattern of Nixon's "warfare of politics" was set. He tried to narrow his senatorial campaign of 1950 against Mrs. Helen Gahagan Douglas to one issue, "simply the choice between freedom and state socialism,"[4] and implied that the latter also meant pro-Russian Communism. Nixon pictured himself as the warrior preserving the American way of life. It was a rough campaign, which, coming on top of the Voorhis contest, left Nixon with the image of "Tricky Dicky," the rabid anticommunist who did not hesitate to use the same tactics of smear and simplification that he accused the communists of using. Indeed, one wonders if mammoth projection was not at work in Nixon. Was he, in fact, defending himself against his own evil impulses by imputing them to others?

Did Nixon believe in what he said, or was his anticommunism largely a matter of practical politics, a convenient way to win? One suspects it was a good deal of both. There was strong personal feeling in Nixon's view of the "enemy." On

82

his Latin American trip in 1958, he talked of the "Communist bully"[5] and described his reaction to the Caracas attack on him as "a feeling of *absolute hatred* for the rough Communist agitators who were driving *children* to this irrational state."[6]* He also talked about "the ruthlessness and determination, the fanaticism of the enemy that we face. That was what I saw in the faces of the mob. *This is really Communism as it is.*"[7]

One cannot help asking what Nixon actually knew about Marxism. (Should we take seriously his comment that "I do not presume to be an expert, and only the experts on Communism, who are sprouting up all over the landscape these days, have single, simple solutions for the problem,"[8] even though Nixon then betrayed his own words by offering rather simple solutions to, and simplifications of, communism?) Did he ever meet any of the leading Marxist theoreticians of Latin America? Did he ever think of comparing lynch mobs in our South with the Caracas mob he faced, and realize that one cannot characterize a whole political setting by such incidents, or, if one can, that both must be characterized equally? Nixon's view of communism was primarily "dramatic" and thus did not allow for such subtleties. His attitude toward communism was best illustrated when, in relation to the Hiss case and the meeting in the Commodore Hotel, he told his television audience, "let me describe the room for you, because it is here that you can see the Communist conspiracy in action . . . twisting and turning and squirming . . . evading and avoiding."[9]

Nixon could not, at least not at this stage of his life, envision communism as anything *but* mob action and individual conspiracy. Can we, however, place this attitude in a larger context? Social scientists have tried to isolate the characteristics

* The San Jose incident of the 1970 election campaign, where Nixon was "attacked" by a rock-throwing mob of young people (whom, in this case, he seems deliberately to have provoked), was a contrived version of the Caracas episode; but the *feelings* involved in both cases seem constant and sincere.

of what they have called an "authoritarian personality."[10] It is worth looking at Nixon's anticommunism in such terms, clearly understanding that there is an element of the authoritarian personality in all of us.

What are the images that Nixon uses? He talks constantly about the threat of the communist "conspiracy." Whatever the reality (and there was some), such extreme concentration on this aspect of communism reveals traces of paranoid fear.[11] For Nixon communism is also an "infection," which can reach almost everyone. It is like the plague, hidden and unsuspected, but capable of striking anyone. As Nixon says of Chambers and Hiss, "They were both idealists. Yet, here are two men of this quality who became infected with Communism, infected with it to the degree that they were willing to run the risk, as they did, of disgrace in order to serve the Communist conspiracy. The fact that this could happen to them shows the potential threat that Communism presents among people of this type throughout the world."[12]

Communism, to Nixon, is "aggressive international Communism . . . on the loose in the world." It is "an insidious evil," engaged in "infiltration of the American government."[13] Communists are "a bunch of rats," and Nixon's only objection to Joe McCarthy's question, "Why worry about being fair when you are shooting rats?" is that you must shoot straight because wild shooting means some of the rats will get away.[14] (And rats carry plague, and plague means infection.) The adjective "communist" is different, but the images of infection and conspiracy are also used by various authoritarian movements to describe the international and domestic "influence" of their enemies.

How much Nixon shares the paranoiac fears that some people defend against by projections and displacements if their own impulses onto an external enemy can be decided only by a prior decision about how much of his rhetoric has been motivated "purely" by political factors. However, we have already seen Nixon, who constantly smeared *his* political opponents, accusing his enemies—communists and crooks—of smearing him. We also wonder about his accusation that his Democratic opponents are "a group of ruthless, cynical seekers after power...."[15] The pattern of projection in Nixon was strong, at least in these early years.*

Yet we must balance this judgment with the knowledge that Nixon began to have a different view of communism after his visit to Moscow and his encounters with *Russian* communists. By 1968, while he still insisted that "the Communist threat is indivisible . . . universal,"[16] he was prepared to say that "the Communists are a very pragmatic people."[17] This is an especially interesting statement in the light of Nixon's concluding remark, in the Mazo-Hess biography, based on an interview with him on May 5, 1968: "I'm a pragmatist with some deep principles that never change."[18] Among these "principles," however, is Nixon's need for an enemy on whom he can project aggressive feelings. Thus, in 1971 as in 1968 North Vietnam is still perceived as the vicious aggressor, part of a continuing world-wide communist conspiracy against a blameless, "free" South Vietnam, whose downfall would herald the loss of freedom everywhere.

The puzzle of how Nixon can have such "extreme" feelings about communism, and yet cordon them off by his pragmatism, is explained to a large extent, I believe, by his subordination of feeling to what he perceives to be the "national interest." Nixon is constantly invoking the good of his party (usually identified with the good of his country) and the good of man-

---

* Clearly, much of Nixon's behavior, even in the area of "smearing" and feeling "smeared," is typical behavior of *all* politicians (which poses some interesting questions on the nature of politics). The problem is to decide whether the degree of feeling raises it to another level and justifies the term "projection."

kind as a justification for his own activities. In the Hiss case he tells us that "more important by far than the fate of the [House Un-American Activities] Committee the national interest required that this investigation go forward."[19] (In the light of my thesis that Nixon partly identified with Chambers, Nixon's analysis of Chambers' motives is interesting: "He had come forward out of necessity, he said, as a kind of duty to warn his country of the scope, strength and danger of the Communist conspiracy in the United States. It would be a great pity if the nation continued to look upon this case as simply a clash of personalities between Hiss and himself. Much more was at stake than what happened to either of them as individuals. Turning to me, he said with great feeling, 'This is what you must get the country to realize.' "[20] Nixon widens the claim further in his writing: "It [the Hiss case] involved the security of the whole nation and the cause of free men everywhere."[21] Similarly, in discussing the Fund case in 1952, and his decision to stay on as Eisenhower's Vice President, Nixon claims that "most important of all, I believed that what I did would affect the future of my country and the cause of peace and freedom for the world."[22]

Is this hyperbole mere rhetoric, or did Nixon sincerely believe what he said? I have no doubt whatever that the latter interpretation is correct. As we have already stressed, Nixon's personal crises were given the status of cosmic events, out of his need to feel himself more adequate. Like most politicians, only more so, Nixon believed in his mission and identified his own self and fortunes with the success of his country. It is part of the secret of *his* political success, since total belief in himself is a means by which a politician convinces others to believe in him. Along with this belief goes the apparently self-effacing notion that, as Nixon told Earl Mazo before 1959, "I don't think that a leader can control to any great extent his destiny." Continuing, Nixon said, "Once a man gets into an

86

important position of leadership—the Presidency, for example—his character can have a great deal of effect on how the stream of events moves one way or the other. He can direct it, but he can't turn it around completely."[23]

We can further see Nixon's sublime belief in the identification of his own interests with the national interest, and, indeed, the interests of all mankind, in such comments as the following: "The Hiss case was the first major crisis of my political life ... [it was] not only an acute personal crisis but ... a vivid case study of the continuing crisis [i.e., Communism] of our times";[24] "While my meeting with Khrushchev might be a personal crisis for me, I recognized that in perspective it was only one episode in the continuing crisis that Mr. Khrushchev and his Communist colleagues are determined to perpetuate through our lifetime";[25] "I recognized the obvious strategy of the Soviets to probe for any weaknesses that might be within me, not unlike their international strategy of probing for soft spots around the world";[26] "I believe in the American dream, because I have seen it come true in my own life";[27] and, lately, Nixon's boastful comment in his acceptance speech to the 1968 Republican National Convention, "My fellow Americans, we make history tonight—not for ourselves alone but for the ages."[28] For better or for worse, Nixon's last claim, and identification, now has the ring of truth about it. His behavior as President of the United States does, in fact as well as in fantasy, affect the behavior of much of the world.

Once President, all of Richard Nixon's "crises" have naturally taken on a vastly more important character than the merely personal, though his "crisis syndrome" is still of crucial significance for Nixon himself. Nixon's one sustained piece of writing is his own *Six Crises*. Throughout that book he is obsessed with the problem of "crisis." Nixon's crisis, however, is far from the psychologist's or psychohistorian's concern with "identity crisis"; for Nixon it is not a question of "finding" himself, but of "testing" his already formed self. The orientation is largely to public events.

Nixon's own initial definition of "crisis" is rather lame. "Life for everyone is a series of crises," he informs us. "A doctor performing a critically difficult operation involving life and death, a lawyer trying an important case, an athlete playing in a championship contest, a salesman competing for a big order, a worker applying for a job or a promotion, an actor on the first night of a new play, an author writing a book—all these situations involve crises for the individuals concerned."[29] Nixon raises the significance of crisis, however, when he continues, "Only when I ran for Congress in 1946 did the meaning of crisis take on sharply expanded dimensions."[30] At this point Nixon jumps personal crises to the hyperbolic level we have discussed before, where, for example, his "Fund" crisis becomes critical to the national interest. In neither of his definitions do we rise above the ordinary, to the sort of real national crisis embodied in one of Nixon's own inspirations: Tom Paine's pamphlet of 1776, *The American Crisis,* with its famous line, "These are the times that try men's souls."[31]

Nixon's own account of how he came to write his *Six Crises* is worth recounting in full, especially since the book itself is one of our main "autobiographical" sources. "Shortly after the election [1960]," he informs us,

I had the honor of sitting by Mrs. Eisenhower at a White House dinner. I told her that one of the reasons I had decided against writing a book was my belief that only the President could write the story of his Administration and that, by comparison, any other account would be incomplete and uninteresting. She answered, "But there are exciting events like your trips to South America and to Russia which only you can tell, and I think people would be interested in reading your account of what really happened."

In April, I visited President Kennedy for the first time since he had taken office. When I told him I was considering the possibility of joining the "literary" ranks, of which he himself is so distinguished a member, he expressed the thought that every public man should write a book at some time in his life, both for the mental discipline and because it tends to elevate him in popular esteem to the respected status of an "intellectual."[32]

The reference to Kennedy is particularly interesting. As others have pointed out, one has the feeling that throughout their political careers, Nixon was measuring and testing himself against this self-assured scion of Eastern wealth and position. The famous television debate was undoubtedly partly motivated by a desire to best Kennedy personally. Moreover, Kennedy was a war hero who had shown remarkable personal courage. It is no accident, then, that Nixon wished to match Kennedy's *Profiles in Courage* with his own *Six Crises*. In it he would prove not only that he had pretension to being an "intellectual," but that he, too, like Kennedy, had courage.

We shall follow up the "intellectual" ambition in a moment, but first we must conclude our account of the genesis of Nixon's book. His close friend and adviser, Adela Rogers St. John, had the greatest influence on Nixon's decision, insisting that he should take time off to write a book. Up until January 20, 1961, Nixon pleaded that he was too busy. The defeat of 1960 left Nixon with time, and when Mrs. St. John sent Ken McCormick of Doubleday & Co. to see him, Nixon was receptive. "I decided," he writes, that

what particularly distinguished my career from that of other public figures was that I had the good (or bad) fortune to be the central figure in several crisis situations with dimensions far beyond personal consideration. I made notes covering a dozen such situations and then selected six of them—the chapter headings of this book— for presentation to McCormick. He approved the concept, told me how easy and enjoyable I would find writing a book to be, and finally convinced me that I should undertake the venture.[33]

At no point did Nixon see his "venture" as an aid in coming to understand himself: "I still did not believe I had reached the point in life for memoir-writing."[34]*

In the book's introduction Nixon makes his gesture toward intellectuality, doing so with an air of humility: "I do not presume to suggest that this is a scholarly treatise on conduct in crisis. The experts will have to judge what contribution my observations may make to a better understanding of that intriguing and vitally important subject."[35] But Nixon then proceeds to offer some generalizations on the topic. Two points are of particular concern to us.

The first is Nixon's conviction that crisis behavior is primarily a "learned" action, and thus available to him. "These attributes [quickness, smartness, boldness] are for the most part acquired and not inherited. . . . Confidence in crisis depends in great part on adequacy of preparation—where preparation is possible."[36] Thus, Nixon's pattern of careful planning and caution works even in the area of personal courage.

The second point is even more revealing. Over and over again, Nixon repeats his main insight about crisis: it is the *aftermath,* not the crisis itself, that is critical for him. At one stage of the Hiss account, he remarks:

> The next morning I learned a fundamental rule of conduct in crises. The point of greatest danger is not in preparing to meet the crisis or fighting the battle; it occurs after the crisis of battle is over, regardless of whether it has resulted in victory or defeat. The individual is spent physically, emotionally and mentally. He lets down. Then if he is confronted with another battle, even a minor skirmish, he is prone to drop his guard and to err in his judgment.[37]

In this particular case what Nixon means is that he went "soft" on Priscilla Hiss.

---

* For my views on the nature of autobiography and its relation to psychohistory, see my article, "Autobiography and Psycho-analysis: Between Truth and Self-Awareness," *Encounter* 35, no. 4 (1970): 28–37.

I subconsciously reacted to the fact that she was a woman, and that the simple rules of courtesy applied. She *played her part* with superb skill. When I asked her to take the oath to tell the truth, she inquired demurely if she could "affirm" rather than "swear." Subtly, she was reminding me of our common Quaker background. . . . She succeeded completely in convincing me that she was nervous and frightened, and I did not press her further. I should have remembered that Chambers had described her as, if anything, a more fanatical Communist than Hiss. I could have made a devastating record had I also remembered that even a woman who happens to be a Quaker and then turns to Communism must be a Communist first and a Quaker second. But I dropped the ball and was responsible for not exploiting what could have been a second breakthrough in the case.[38]

(It is worth noting Nixon's awareness that Mrs. Hiss was playing on their common Quaker background, a fact he has admitted to himself vis-à-vis Chambers; his imagery of the football game—"I dropped the ball"—is also significant.)

Nixon then connects the personal with the political interest.

I was never to make that same error again. In the years ahead I would never forget that where the battle against Communism is concerned, victories are never final so long as the Communists are still able to fight. There is never a time when it is safe to relax or let down. When you have won one battle is the time you should step up your effort to win another—until final victory is achieved.[39]

Since we are interested mainly in the personal aspect, Nixon's most important remark comes when he says, "I experienced a sense of let down which is difficult to describe or *even to understand.*"[40] Can we understand what happened better than Nixon himself?

We must ask what functions crisis performed for Nixon. As he perceived it, on the public or political level, the successful handling of what he calls a crisis enhances a leader in the eyes of his followers. For example, the Caracas "crisis" boosted Nixon's popularity greatly. As he put it, "in June 1958, just one month after my return from South America, the Gallup

Poll showed me leading Adlai Stevenson for the first time, and running neck-and-neck against John F. Kennedy. It was the high point of my political popularity up to that time."[41] Nixon generalizes that "It is the crisis, itself, more than the merits of the engagement which rallies people to a leader. Moreover, when the leader handles the crisis with success, the public support he receives is even greater."[42] One cannot help but assume that the Cambodian episode, for example, was undertaken with this precept in mind; Nixon, of course, did not expect it to backfire.

It ought not to surprise us that Nixon projects some of his own attitudes, in this area as in others, onto the Communists. At the start of the chapter on Khrushchev he informs us that "Communism creates and uses crisis as a weapon."[43] Later in the chapter Nixon elaborates: "They [Communists] use crisis as a weapon, as a tactic in their all-front, all-out struggle."[44]

As we know, Nixon defines a leader as one able to act in a crisis. He also stresses that a leader without crisis is almost a contradiction in terms. As he said about Eisenhower: he "demonstrated a trait that I believe all great leaders have in common: they thrive on challenge; they are at their best when the going is hardest. When life is routine, they become bored; when they have no challenge, they tend to wither and die or to go to seed."[45] One of Nixon's concluding remarks to his chapter on the campaign of 1960 is even more revealing: "But probably the greatest magnet of all is that those who have known great crisis—its challenge and tension, its victory and defeat—can never become adjusted to a more leisurely and orderly pace. They have drunk too deeply of the stuff which really makes life exciting and worth living to be satisfied with the froth."[46] In the light of all the foregoing, can one help concluding that Nixon, like the communists, "uses crisis as a weapon, as a tactic" and will so create and use it in the future when "tactics" call for it?

The above discussion explores the "public" dimension of

Nixon's crisis. But we need to go deeper and try to understand his "letdown" feeling. We begin to approach a fuller understanding if we look at "crisis" in relation to decisiveness. Decisiveness is obviously a serious problem for Nixon. In discussing Eisenhower's heart attack, Nixon makes two revealing statements:

This was far different from any other crisis I had faced in my life and had to be handled differently. I had always believed in meeting a crisis head-on. The difficult period is reaching a decision, but once that has been done, the carrying-out of the decision is easier than the making of it. In meeting any crisis in life, one must either fight or run away. But one must do something. Not knowing how to act or not being able to act is what tears your insides out [47]

And, a few pages later: "For me . . . this period continued to be one which drained my emotional as well as physical energies, for it was, above all, a period of indecision."[48]

Interestingly enough, Nixon accused Stevenson of being "a man plagued with indecisions who could speak beautifully but could not act decisively."[49] Toward Eisenhower, Nixon had ambivalent feelings which he found it hard to suppress. For example, Nixon says that "what had happened during the past week had not shaken my faith in Eisenhower. If, as some of my associates believe, he appeared indecisive, I put the blame not on him but on his lack of experience in political warfare."[50] Later on, he declares emphatically:

Eisenhower was a man of decision. As General Walter Bedell Smith had pointed out in his book, *Eisenhower's Six Great Decisions* [another inspiration for Nixon's *Six Crises*?], he never did anything rashly. Sometimes he took more time to decide an issue than some of his eager lieutenants thought necessary, but invariably, when the line was drawn and the lonely responsibility for making the right decision rested solely with him, he came up with the right answer.[51]

After his television program about the Fund, Nixon said to Eisenhower, "if you think I should stay on or get off, I think you should say so either way. The great trouble here is the indecision."[52]

Nixon, however, had to wrestle not only with the problem of indecisiveness, his own and that of others, but also with the problem of holding fast to a decision once taken. We have already noted his "decision" to retire from politics after his term as Vice President ended in 1957, a decision that was reinforced by being put on paper and tucked into his wallet—and then was repudiated promptly in 1960. Earlier, in 1956, during the "Dump Nixon" movement, we are told that "on a Wednesday he told two or three friends he would call a press conference the next day to make an announcement of retirement from public life";[53] naturally, he was talked out of this "decision." So, too, although he promised his friend, Elmer Bobst, that he "wouldn't run" for governor of California, Nixon changed his mind. The high spot in this pattern was his 1962 "retirement" speech to the press (after his gubernatorial defeat), and then his Lazarus-like resurrection in 1968. Clearly, the really decisive member of the Nixon family was Pat.

Since Nixon is plagued with the torments of decision and indecision in a "crisis" situation, we can begin to see why he feels "letdown" after his emotional fight is over. Even when he has made a decision, his ambivalences are so great that he is drained of energy and inwardly unsure whether he would be able to hold to his own decision.

An even more important reason for his feeling letdown is related to Nixon's attitudes about aggression. Nixon seems to have enormously ambivalent feelings about the release of hostile emotions, probably dating back to his mother's injunctions, and consequently experiences strong, though unconscious, feelings of guilt after their release. Moreover, because of the tremendous effort of control needed to fight effectively and to harden himself for a struggle (*which does not come naturally to him,* even though events and his party have cast him in this role) and because of his constant personal need to "test" himself, Nixon runs the danger of going "soft." This moment of weakness is, therefore, additionally threatening to him.

What is the evidence for this combined thesis? In one of Nixon's most revealing comments he says:

> The most difficult period in one of these incidents is not in handling the situation at the time. The difficult task is with your reactions after it is all over. I get a real let down after one of these issues. Then I begin to think of what bums they are. You also get the sense that you licked them . . . though they really poured it on. Then you try to catch yourself . . . in statements and actions . . . to be a generous winner, if you have won.[54]

Here, again, the term "letdown" is used. If one's opponents are "bums," then one is clearly justified in fighting them without quarter. But, then, the guilt sets in, and one catches oneself and tries to be a generous winner.

Since becoming President, Nixon has obliged me by using the term "bums" again. On May 1, 1970, he underlined the significance of the term for his psychic economy when he publicly labeled campus radicals protesting his Vietnam policy as "bums," a term we are told that he had been known to apply to them frequently in private. "You see these bums," he said, "you know blowing up the campuses today are the luckiest people in the world, going to the greatest universities, and here they are burning up the books, storming around about this issue." Opposed to these "bums," in Nixon's psychic drama, were the good characters. "Then out there," he went on, "we have *kids* who are just doing their duty. They stand tall and they are proud. I am sure they are scared. *I was when I was there.* But when it really comes down to it, they stand up and, boy, you have to talk up to these *men.* They are going to do fine and we have to stand in back of them."[55]

These statements are enormously revealing of the "real" Richard Nixon and bear close reading. They show how "overdetermined" (see p. 159ff. for a discussion of overdetermination) his emotions actually are in this matter. It is extraordinary to find a photograph of Richard Nixon, with his girl friend Ola-Florence, on Dress-up Day at Whittier High School back in 1930, in which Nixon is masquerading as a bum-panhandler![56] Add to this Nixon's own recollection that his grandmother, whom he admired enormously, "was always taking care of every tramp that came along the road, just like my own mother, too . . . she always was taking somebody in."[57]

Why, then, did Nixon in later life turn against "bums?" Faintly through these accounts, we see a boy who wanted desperately to be "taken in," cared for by his mother and grandmother, spoiled, and given things freely (was the memory of his brother wishing for a horse also a displacement, in part?). At some point in college, presumably, this became a terribly threatening image to Nixon, a "negative identity" that he had to shun, as he turned to enormous hard work and self-control. The "controlled" Nixon won out in his relations with Ola-Florence, even if this necessitated an "uncontrolled" outburst of temper. He won a final victory, I suspect, in the OPA experience in Washington. When he was confronted in 1970 by "spoiled" college students, who, in addition to fighting against him, had had everything that he had earlier to deny to himself, the "controlled" Nixon surfaced again. Small wonder that Nixon could justify his aggression against "bums": the aggression was as much against a part of himself as against his external enemies.

Ambivalent about aggression, tormented by indecision in crises, Nixon alternates between denial of aggressive intent and glorification of the hard struggle. Typically, he identifies himself with the nation and denies any aggressive desires in either. Thus, he tells us that "Khrushchev does not need to be convinced of our good intentions. He knows we are not aggressors and do not threaten the security of the Soviet Union." Again, "It was my belief that Khrushchev knew that our intentions were peaceful."[58] The fact that Khrushchev and the Russians might remember the American intervention in the Russian Civil

War, the American willingness, in part, to have Germany invade Russia, and so forth was all written off by Nixon as merely an "act" on Khrushchev's part. In this denial of his own aggressive intent, and this refusal to recognize his opponent's real fears of it, Nixon seems at one with much of America's recent self-image.

While denying aggressive intent, Nixon could glorify fighting and the hard masculine qualities that necessarily go with it. Thus, Nixon could compare Khrushchev and Eisenhower in an interesting conjunction of adjectives: "Men like you and President Eisenhower," he told Khrushchev, "are tough, reasonable men who are not soft or frightened. . . ."[59] Or, speaking in praise of the average Russian: "there was a steel-like quality, a cold determination, a tough, amoral ruthlessness which somehow had been instilled into every one of them."[60] Nixon constantly asked himself, "How did we stack up against the kind of fanatically dedicated men I had seen in the past ten days?"[61] We can see how Nixon wished to answer this question for himself, as well as for the American people, in the following, most revealing, comment about his career in New York after the 1962 defeat:

New York is very cold and very ruthless and very exciting, and therefore, an interesting place to live. It has many great disadvantages but also many advantages. The main thing, it is a place where you can't slow down—a fast track. Any person tends to vegetate unless he is moving on a fast track. New York is a very challenging place to live. You have to bone up to keep alive in the competition here.[62]

Such a statement must be placed in the context of Nixon's parental models: the mother who did not wish him to enter the "warfare of politics," and the father with "his fierce competitive drive." Is it any wonder that Nixon has a problem making the decision to fight, to release *his* competitive drive, and that he feels a letdown after the semiforbidden impulses have been unleashed? But having indicated Nixon's ambivalence in this matter, we must conclude with the observation that Nixon did, indeed, gain strength from his difficulties. Like his Russian foes, he learned to "steel" himself, and to reject the softer, debilitating, and feminine impulses that threaten him so fearfully—for the simple reason that they are so strongly contained within him. Once again, out of "weakness" Nixon can be said to have drawn "strength."

We must briefly discuss one particular crisis in Nixon's life a bit further. This continuous crisis, involving his relationship to President Eisenhower, unfolds in half of the six crises in Nixon's book: "The Fund," "The Heart Attack," and "The Campaign of 1960." Much of Nixon's mature life, until the present, has circled about Eisenhower: it was Eisenhower who picked him out of obscurity to be his running mate in 1952, almost dumped him in the Fund controversy that then erupted, allowed a "Dump Nixon" movement to spread in 1956, almost presented Nixon with the Presidency itself because of his heart attack in 1955 and stroke in 1957, and played an ambiguous role in Nixon's own campaign for President in 1960. On a more intimate level the two families were united by the marriage of Ike's grandson David to Nixon's daughter Julie. On the deepest personal level Eisenhower presented Nixon with a crisis of feeling, involving emotions about Ike as a beloved and admired father figure, to whom death wishes as both father and President became attached. These, we need hardly add, would be on the unconscious level.

The evidence that Eisenhower was a father figure is strong. At one point in discussing the fund, Nixon says of Eisenhower's attitude, "I must admit that it made me feel like the little boy caught with jam on his face."[63] Again, further on, he repeats the little boy image: "Chotiner [his adviser], particularly, insisted that I not allow myself to be put in the position of going to Eisenhower like a little boy to be taken to the woodshed, properly punished, and then restored to a place of dignity"[64] (and we remember Nixon's possible "spankings" at home). On a slightly different note Eisenhower is a commanding authority figure, and Nixon remarks that "despite his great capacity for friendliness, he also had a quality of reserve which, at least subconsciously, tended to make a visitor feel like a junior officer coming in to see the commanding General."[65] Given Nixon's feelings of "little boy" and "junior officer" (Nixon was, in fact, a Lt. Commander at the end of World War II), we can understand better his tears when in 1952 Eisenhower, the "father," finally accepted him back on the team:

"General, you didn't need to come out to the airport," was all I could think to say.

"Why not?": he said with a broad grin, "you're my boy."

We walked to the head of the ramp, posed for photographers, and then rode together to the Wheeling stadium. I was still so surprised by his unexpected gesture of coming to meet me that I found myself riding on his right as the car pulled away from the airport. I apologized for what I, with my Navy training, knew was an inexcusable breach of political as well as military protocol, and tried to change places with him. He put his hand on my shoulder and said, "Forget it. No one will know the difference with all the excitement out there."[66]

No one "out there" might know, but Nixon "knew" inwardly that he had usurped Eisenhower's place and fulfilled a forbidden, though perfectly natural, wish. Nixon would have had to be inhuman not to have mixed feelings toward the man who placed him just one heart beat away from the highest office in the land. The fact that Nixon behaved with exemplary restraint during Ike's incapacity suggests both shrewd political judgment on the conscious level and tremendous ambivalence on the unconscious level. Death wishes are generally compounded of many parts: love for the potential victim and anticipation of great loss, secret satisfaction at his removal, guilt for this suppressed feeling and the gladness one experiences at surviving him, and so forth. Nixon's reaction to the news of Eisenhower's heart attack shows, first, denial and, then, numbing. According to Mazo and Hess, he reacted as follows when told of Eisenhower's condition:

"My God!" Nixon whispered hoarsely. He caught his breath, then proceeded to tell Hagerty that heart attacks are not necessarily serious any more, that victims frequently recover completely.

"I don't see how I could describe those first few minutes except as a complete shock," he recalls. "I remember going into my living room and sitting down in a chair and not saying anything or really thinking of anything for at least five or ten minutes. For quite a while I didn't even think to tell Pat, who was upstairs."

The numbness receded gradually. Nixon went back to the telephone and called Deputy Attorney General William P. Rogers.[67]

The alternating love-hate relationship put Nixon through the emotional wringer.* First, Eisenhower had chosen Nixon as his heir by selecting him for Vice President in 1952. Then, he had shown no faith in his choice and seemed willing to drop him before the Checkers speech.

Worse, Eisenhower awakened all of Nixon's problems about indecision; the situation was compounded by the fact that Nixon had to repress almost all his aggressive feelings toward Eisenhower. How strong these aggressive impulses were we can see from Nixon's one outbreak, when Eisenhower stated that he did not think that he, Eisenhower, should make the decision about Nixon staying on the ticket. According to Mazo and Hess, "At this Nixon stiffened and said sternly, 'There comes a time in a man's life when he has to fish or cut bait.' (Actually, his words were stronger.)"[68] Nixon then gave a speech that in many ways tried to turn the tables on Ike; the Checkers speech was, in fact, a highly aggressive defense.[69]

---

* Cf. Emmet John Hughes' devastating comment about the relationship: "The fact is that no one in public life may have done more to seal Richard Nixon's sense of personal isolation than Dwight Eisenhower. For the General-President acted as a political father to his official successor with roughly the enthusiasm that most men show in situations of wholly unplanned paternity." (*New York Times,* April, 4, 1971, p. 70.)

Incidentally, in my initial analysis I added the phrase, "we can certainly guess at Eisenhower's reaction to such a statement," and put in parenthesis in the text, "possibly anal in the actual words." Then, I added a footnote:

Quite a while after writing this paragraph, I came across some confirmation of my guess as to the actual phrase used by Nixon. Alsop, *Nixon and Rockefeller,* p. 63, claims "three people who should know" have Nixon saying "pee or get off the pot." My own hunch is still that the language was even stronger than this. After all, one of Nixon's triumphs in college was bringing in a "four holer" to his fraternity.

As I had guessed, the actual words *were* stronger. Additional information, now available, confirms my guess. Every once in a while, in psychohistory, as in psychoanalysis, one makes a prediction as to evidence that will appear—and, lo and behold, it does! It is a very gratifying feeling when this occurs, like fitting the right piece into a jigsaw puzzle. What Nixon actually said on the telephone, in the presence of a number of listeners, was "General, there comes a time in matters like this when you've either got to shit or get off the pot."[70]

Psychohistory, as we shall see in more detail in the last section, is primarily a retrodictive rather than a truly predictive discipline. That is, psychohistory explains past events partly on the basis of "predicting" the appearance of confirming material already existing but not yet discovered. This "prediction" of forthcoming evidence is occasionally made possible because of evidence of an overdetermined pattern. In this case my "hunch" was based on my feeling that Nixon had a strong quality of anality (a quality we shall discuss independently, later); therefore, I believed that he would erupt in these terms in a moment of great anger. If I had known at the time that the slogan for the college social club that Nixon had founded was, "Beans, Brawn, Brains and Bowels" (Beans have a double *entendre* related to Bowels), I would have been even surer in my guess. Even without this knowledge at the time, however, I suspected that the man with the "iron butt," as his friends described him, would resort to anal language. It was, and is, a trivial "prediction"; it is, however, indicative of the sort of pattern one begins to discern through the use of the psychohistorical method.

Knowing the actual words coming from Eisenhower's "junior officer," we can speculate with some confidence that Ike's enthusiasm for his "boy," Nixon, was always tempered by the memory of that phrase. Shortly after the Checkers affair, however, Eisenhower took Nixon back into his good graces, and Eisenhower's praise pushed Nixon all the way over to the other side of his feelings. After the Checkers speech, we are told, Eisenhower said that "as a 'warrior,' he had never seen 'courage' to surpass that shown by Nixon . . . and in a showdown fight he preferred 'one courageous honest man' at his side to 'a whole boxcar full of pussy-footers.' "[71] This must have been music to Nixon's ears, in view of his concern for courage and his desire to be a warrior in politics, according to his father's inspiration.

But Nixon's emotional ordeals with Eisenhower were far from over. The heart attack imposed the next strain. There is an unsuspected psychological aspect to the story Nixon tells about Ike's grandson: "David, the President's oldest and favorite grandchild, provided a pleasant interlude when he came into the room. Hagerty introduced me as 'the Vice President of the United States.' David took a second look and said, 'The Vice President, wow!' Then he turned to his grandfather and said, 'Ike, I didn't know there were two Presidents.' "[72] Obviously, there was room for only one President, and as soon as Eisenhower recovered he resumed the full powers of his office. At that point he expressed no appreciation to Nixon for being the second President. As Nixon remarks, "He had also spoken or written to me personally of his appreciation after each of my trips abroad. But after this most difficult assignment of all— treading the tightrope during his convalescence from the heart attack—there was no personal thank you."[73] That Nixon was hurt is clear, even though he quickly adds, "Nor was one needed or expected. After all, we both recognized that I had only done what a Vice President should do when the President is ill."[74] (If that is so, why does Nixon mention it?)

A year later the same pattern reappeared. Indeed, Nixon's anguish over the 1956 Vice Presidential nomination was even greater. We are told that "one of [Nixon's friends] who suffered through the whole emotional ordeal with Nixon said Eisenhower's reluctance to come out flatly and ask Nixon to be his running mate was 'one of the greatest hurts of his [Nixon's] career.' "[75] Nixon explains it as follows:

I considered it improper for me to indicate my desires until his plans, which were paramount, were made clear. I couldn't say: "Look, Mr. President, I want to run." He never put the question to me in quite the right way for that response. If he said, "Dick, I want you to be the (vice presidential) candidate, if you want to be," I would have accepted, thanked him, and that would have been that.[76]

Further on, Nixon writes:

It seemed to me that it was like the fund controversy all over again. But *then* Eisenhower had not known me well and had every justification for not making a decision with regard to keeping me on the ticket until all the facts were in. *Now,* he had had an opportunity to evaluate my work over the past three years, and particularly during the period after the heart attack. If he still felt, under these circumstances, that he wanted me on the ticket only if I insisted on seeking the post, I concluded he should have someone else in whom he had more confidence as his running mate.[77]

In this mood Nixon even goes so far as to make an indirect accusation: "Letters and calls flooded my office charging that the President was being 'ungrateful,' particularly in view of my conduct during the period since his heart attack."[78]

The extraordinary thing is that, after all this, Nixon, unable to bear the implied aggression, ends up taking upon himself the blame for what happened. Eisenhower, the father figure, can do no wrong. After finally making the decision—a deci-

sion Eisenhower would not make—to ask Eisenhower to keep
him on the ticket, Nixon concludes with a roundabout admission of his *own* failure:

And so ended the personal crisis involved in my decision to be a
candidate for Vice President in 1956. In retrospect, it was a minor
crisis, for the outcome really never was in doubt. Yet it was part of
the much more serious heart attack crisis for me—the aftermath
when my guard was down. I would otherwise not have been as
sensitive about Eisenhower's attitude toward my candidacy, and
would have resolved the situation myself much sooner. The significance, at least for me, once again was that the most dangerous
period of a crisis is not the preparation or the battle itself, but the
aftermath when one's normal reaction, after having mobilized all
one's emotions and physical resources to fight the battle, is to relax.
If you cannot take the time off to let your system relax and re-
charge normally, then you must be alert to the fact that your
temper will be short and your judgment less acute than normally.
During the trying months when the President had lain ill, I had
expanded my energies not only in a heavier work schedule but in
treading a tightrope of political diplomacy. Then, before I could
recover my equilibrium, I found myself on political tenterhooks and
I reacted with less than my best judgment.[79]

There was one last twinge of the filial nerve. In 1960 Nixon
was at last about to be his own man, running for the Presidency himself. At this point Eisenhower, advertently or inadvertently, made a major blooper. Asked at a Presidential press
conference on August 24 "to give us an example of a major
idea of his [Nixon's] that you adopted . . . ," he replied, "If
you give me a week, I might think of one."[80] Nevertheless, and
perhaps in a repentant mood, Eisenhower offered to aid Nixon
actively in his campaign, promising to serve as "a soldier in
the ranks." Many of Nixon's advisors and assistants were jubi-
lant, knowing the lift that Ike's appeals to the American people
would bring to the ticket. But to almost everyone's surprise
and consternation, Nixon refused the General's offer. While
expressing his gratitude, he thought that it might not be proper
or wise for Eisenhower to undertake an exhausting barnstorm-

ing tour of the country. Difficult as it was to resist Eisenhower's offer, Nixon said, he was, in fact, declining it.

Theodore White and others have suggested that Nixon was rebelling against Ike, the father figure. "The Nixon people," White wrote, "and Nixon himself, who had been treated like boys for so many years by the Eisenhower people, now apparently itched to operate on their own." This psychological explanation certainly hits close to the mark for Nixon, though it has to be supplemented by the very real possibility that he was also concerned about the health of the man he admired so much. Given Nixon's feelings about being the "junior officer," Eisenhower's "soldier in the ranks" offer must have awakened strange, disturbing feelings in Nixon, and the memory of the inept "give me a week" response must have left him with some trepidation as to how Eisenhower might behave in his "lowly" role.

There is little need for further speculation. Nixon's victory on his own in 1968 undoubtedly was a successful achievement of the position of primacy, without the replacement of the father implicit in the 1960 campaign. There was also no need for death wishes—or fears. (Nixon's own father had died in 1956.) In fact, the marriage of David Eisenhower to Nixon's daughter Julie now put *Nixon* in the role of father figure, and David's break with family tradition, entering the Navy instead of the Army—and therefore emulating his father-in-law—confirmed the switch in roles. There is something touching, and terribly revealing, in Nixon's comment to David at the Navy swearing-in ceremony: "I've got a couple of old uniforms you can use."[81] In this area I believe that we do have a "new Nixon," released from old emotions. I suspect that his nomination of the unknown Spiro Agnew was in part a replaying, in reverse, of his own nomination from obscurity by Eisenhower. The assignment of Agnew to the "low road" of hatchet man, while Nixon strolled along the "high road," offers some confirmation of this hypothesis. In any case Nixon was no longer Eisenhower's or anybody else's "little boy." We can postulate that, as he stood on the threshold of achieving his ambition to be President, Nixon had passed through this "crisis" in his life—in this unsuspected sense, an "identity crisis"—and had finally come to a kind of maturity.

# 5

---

# THE
# PRESIDENTIAL
# NIXON

★★★★★★★★★★★★★★★★★★★★★★★★★★★★★★★★★★★★★★★★★★

**W**HAT are the characteristics of Nixon as President? How can we relate the projections of his personal drama to the political arena and to his conception of the Presidential role?

Preliminary to our effort to establish this relation, we must remind ourselves of a difficulty to be borne constantly in mind. How are we to distinguish what is particularly personal to Nixon from what is characteristic of all politicians? This is a sticky issue for all psychohistorical work. The need to believe well of oneself, to think of oneself as principled and fair, and to avoid self-examination seems to be characteristic of politicians as a group; as the journalist David Broder suggested to me, perhaps it is a minimum requirement of their egos to sustain them against "the terrific competitive pressures of their profession." So, too, simple political necessity often forces politicians to take public positions during a campaign diametrically opposed to what they know to be right and truthful. Once again, the question of "degree" arises. More than this, however, the question of "fit" also is raised: the way in which an individual's personality allows him to be a "typical" politician (Adlai Stevenson obviously had difficulties in this respect), and the ways in which the behavior of politicians "fits" the expectations of their constituents.

## Images of a President

Keeping this issue in mind in our attempt at a closer look at his behavior after 1968, we need directly to confront the question: What is Nixon's own image of himself? Such a self-image will bear immediately on his own role expectations as President, as well as determine how he views other Presidents, such as Wilson or Lincoln, as models for himself. Nixon's first self-image is that he is a "big," a "great" man. In the introduction to *Six Crises* he says, "We often hear it said that truly 'big' men are at their best in handling big affairs, and that they falter and fail when confronted with petty irritations—with crises which are, in other words, essentially personal." A few paragraphs further on, Nixon comments: "No one really knows what he is capable of until he is tested to the full by events over which he may have no control. That is why this book is an account not of great men but rather of great events—and how one man responded to them."[1] Nixon's "great events" include the Fund controversy, Eisenhower's heart attack, the visit to Caracas, and his encounter with Khrushchev—hardly events that will figure in future history books—yet implicit in the book is his belief that, having handled these "big affairs" well, he is a "big" man.

During the 1960 campaign Nixon had explicitly compared himself with a great President, Abraham Lincoln, and had suggested that the great events confronting him, Nixon, were even greater than those of 1860: "One hundred years ago, in this very city, Abraham Lincoln was nominated for President. . . . The question then was freedom for the slaves and survival for the nation. The question now is freedom for all mankind and the survival of civilization."[2] The hyperbole about the survival of civilization is partly the usual political rhetoric, but it is also a reflection of Nixon's self-confidence, a vital ingredient for any politician.

What emerges overwhelmingly from a reading of Nixon's own writings, as well as the various biographies about him, is Nixon's ability, at least on the surface, to think well of himself, to believe he is always acting fairly, and to deny to himself almost any of his nasty, aggressive feelings. Such a picture of himself, of course, serves valuable political functions: it encourages voters to take the same view of him, it protects him from conscious doubt of his own motives, and so forth. For example, he made the following statement, which demonstrates considerable psychological insight, but then failed to see its applicability to himself. "From considerable experience in observing witnesses on the stand," he tells us, "I had learned that those who are lying or *trying to cover up something* generally make a common mistake—they tend to overact, to overstate their case."[3] This comes from the man who could say about his vicious campaign against Voorhis that it "was a very honest debate on the issues." This is the same Nixon who could say throughout the 1940s, 1950s, and early 1960s that communism was an indivisible monolith, and then say, without blushing, in a 1968 interview that "I don't see the Communist world as one world. I see the shades of gray. I see it as a multicolor thing."[4] So, too, Nixon, who used the smear against Voorhis, Mrs. Douglas, and Adlai Stevenson, could complain about a *New York Post* story insinuating wrongdoing in a Nixon political fund in the following terms: "After all, I had come into this 1952 campaign well prepared, I thought, for any political smear that could be directed at me. After what my opponents had thrown at me in my campaign for the House and Senate, and after the almost unbelievably vicious assaults I had survived during the Hiss case, I thought I had been through the worst."[5] Nixon, one of the most pragmatic and expedient of politicians—witness his 1968 alliance with the Southern politicians, such as Strom Thurmond—could sincerely state:

My philosophy has always been: don't lean with the wind. Don't do what is politically expedient. Do what your instinct tells you is right. Public opinion polls are useful if a politician uses them only to learn approximately what the people are thinking, so that he can talk to them more intelligently. The politician who sways with

**111**

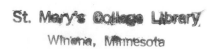

the polls is not worth his pay. And I believe the people eventually catch up with the man who merely tells them what he thinks they want to hear.[6]

The same Nixon who was to appoint Agnew as his running mate in 1968, could state in 1961, when writing *Six Crises,* that the Vice President should be selected as a real deputy, able to be President if necessary: "This being true," he informs us, "it will also bolster the new political trend of selecting capable men as vice presidential nominees, men to whom the presidential nominee would be willing to turn over his duties during a period of disability, rather than the selection of men solely on geographical, factional, or party appeasement considerations."[7] It is true that there is some evidence of Nixon's admiration for Agnew as a strong man, who is therefore qualified to succeed him, but the bulk of the evidence points to Agnew's selection out of more mundane "appeasement" considerations. One can also argue that changing circumstances make for changing views, and Nixon has merely adapted to reality, as in his views on communism. I cannot accept this explanation. Nixon's ability to believe in the rightness, the *total* rightness, of whatever he is saying at the moment is so pervasive, and so in tune with what is expedient, that I see no grounds for believing in any real change of principles or perception of reality. For example, Nixon really believed what he said in the 1960 campaign:

On this and every other issue, the admonition I gave to some of those who had a tendency to let their eagerness to appeal to voters overrule their judgment on the substance of issues went something like this: "We must always assume that we are going to win this election. And I do not want to say anything or do anything during the campaign that I will not be able to live with as President."[8]

Yet the aftermath of 1968, as well as the pattern of Nixon's political life before, show us otherwise (for example, Nixon's espousal of black capitalism). The high point in this double talk came when Nixon described his last television debate with

Kennedy in 1960 over the Cuban issue. According to Nixon, Kennedy accused the Republicans of do-nothingism and advocated aid to rebel forces in Cuba, *knowing* (he had been briefed) that the CIA had been training Cuban exiles to invade Cuba. Nixon explained how he rose to this crisis:

What could I do? One course would be simply to state that what Kennedy was advocating as a new policy was already being done, had been adopted as a policy as a result of my direct support, and that Kennedy was endangering the security of the whole operation by his public statement. But this would be, for me, an utterly irresponsible act: it would disclose a secret operation and completely destroy its effectiveness.

There was only one thing I could do. The covert operation had to be protected at all costs. I must not even suggest by implication that the United States was rendering aid to rebel forces in and out of Cuba. In fact, I must go to the other extreme: I must attack the Kennedy proposal to provide such aid as wrong and irresponsible because it would violate our treaty commitments.[9]

Then came the climax. Nixon said in the debate:

"I think that Senator Kennedy's policies and recommendations for the handling of the Castro regime are probably the most dangerously irresponsible recommendations that he's made during the course of this campaign."

But I could not say why. Instead, I took this tack: ". . . if we were to follow that recommendation . . . we would lose all of our friends in Latin America, we would probably be condemned in the United Nations, and we would not accomplish our objective. . . . It would be an open invitation for Mr. Khrushchev . . . to come into Latin America and to engage us in what would be a civil war and possibly even worse than that."[10]

How, one wonders, could Nixon *possibly* say this, knowing even better than Kennedy that this was *exactly* what the United States intended to do? And, having said it, how could he then expect us to believe him when he claimed, "I do not want to say anything or do anything during the campaign that I will not be able to live with as President."

This, however, is the same self-righteous Nixon who told Khrushchev that this country is completely nonaggressive and spelled out "in detail that the United States had fought in two great world wars and had never exacted any territorial gains or reparations and that the United States had no designs on world conquest."[11] Okinawa was presumably unknown to Nixon, who served in the United States Navy in the Pacific. Of course, when Khrushchev says that "the Soviet Union wanted to live in peace and friendship—but was fully prepared to protect itself in war,"[12] we are expected to treat this as complete, conscious fabrication.

Fundamentally, Nixon is in my sense an uncritical man. He does not really examine and weigh the validity of his statements (would this be dysfunctional for a politician, showing him lacking self-confidence?). Thus, we are told by Mazo and Hess that Nixon "never shared the belief of some in the Eisenhower administration that 'Communism to McCarthy was a racket.' Nixon felt that the Senator 'believed what he was doing very deeply.' "[13] (Yet Nixon knew that McCarthy had exhibited no knowledge of, or antipathy toward, communism before his West Virginia "numbers" speech.) Similarly, Nixon mentioned that the House Un-American Activities Committee

had been widely condemned as a "Red-baiting" group, habitually unfair and irresponsible, whose investigations had failed to lead to a single conviction of anyone against whom charges had been made at its hearings. It was, the critics said, doing more of a disservice to the country because of its abridgement of civil liberties than any alleged services it might be rendering in uncovering Communist subversives.[14]

But at no point did he admit the justice of the charges.

The uncritical Nixon, however, sees himself in a very different light from the one I have cast on him. For example, he commented about his performance in his first television debate with Kennedy:

114

I had concentrated too much on substance and not enough on appearance. I should have remembered that "a picture is worth a thousand words." I would be the first to recognize that I have many weaknesses as a political candidate, but one of my strengths is that I try to be my own severest critic.[15]

Obviously, Nixon's concept of criticism is in no way related to my use of the term "criticism."

In general, Nixon's basic vision of himself is as a high-principled, fair-minded man (of greatness), who is constantly being unfairly attacked and smeared by his opponents (mainly communists and crooks), and who is his own severest critic. Much of this self-image, we must admit, corresponds to the image of self-righteousness projected by America as a whole; this correspondence is undoubtedly a part of Nixon's political success.

Who, then, is the "real" Richard Nixon, as distinct from the one he sees, and how has he actually acted as President? Nixon, we have been saying, envisions himself as principled and strong. However, he has not considered other sides of himself. Outstanding among them is what I shall call Nixon's fear of passivity. He is afraid of being acted upon, of being inactive, of being soft, of being thought impotent, and of being dependent on any one else. Nixon himself gives surface acknowledgment to this trait. When asked about any special affinity he had to Teddy Roosevelt, he replied, "I guess I'm like him in one way only: I like to be in the arena. I have seen those who have nothing to do—I could be one of them if I wanted—the people just lying around at Palm Beach. Nothing could be more pitiful." Wills, who reports this interview, tells us that "his voice had contempt in it, not pity."[16]

This is in part the same feeling evoked by the image of "bums" as used by Nixon. We must remember, however, that as a little boy Nixon "played" the role of bum himself, only

115

to reject it later with "contempt." He was notorious for lying around and dreaming and wished badly to have "his mother to do things for him." Suffice it to say that on the unconscious level, we have numerous examples of Nixon's fear of passivity and softness. He is constantly talking about an enemy, such as the Soviets, probing for weakness, for soft spots in him (and thus America). To defend us and himself, Nixon must deny he is "soft" on communism, or Castro, or anything else. In the General Beadle State College speech Nixon had to attack "the old, familiar, *self-indulgent* (my italics) cry for the easy way" and demand, instead, "hard discipline."

Nixon's need for and admiration of "strong" women has already been underlined. He expresses what seems an inordinate admiration for this same quality in men. In an interview with some women correspondents on March 13, 1971, Nixon commented on the sort of advisors a President needed: "does he have around him people who are standing with him, people that are strong, people who aren't panicking . . . somebody who brings serenity, calmness or strength into the room." One such advisor, it appears, is John Newton Mitchell, a "strong" man, seemingly imperturbable, free of doubts, advocating a "get tough" policy. Spiro Agnew, it seems, was picked partly because he impressed Nixon on first sight as somebody who was sure of himself, who was without weakness, who's "got it." John Connolly, now Secretary of the Treasury, appears to be the latest addition to Nixon's circle of "strong men." (Though Nixon does not mention this, he appears also to need "weaker" men, such as his friend, Robert Finch; in fact, Nixon's view of his Cabinet, with the recent exception of Connolly, seems not to allow for "strong" men there. Such balancing of strong and weak corresponds with Nixon's own ambivalence.)

There can be no question that Nixon's concern with strength corresponds with the feelings of the American electorate. When Theodore White circulated in the crowd at a Nixon prenomination speech, he heard the assembled Republicans muttering, "He's strong . . . that's why I'm for him," "I like the way he talks . . . he sounds strong."[17] Whatever the reality, it seems a candidate or a President must sound "strong." He must also make his listeners feel somehow that they, too, participate in strength. Nixon accurately appealed to his audience when he remarked in an Air Force Academy speech (June 1969) that, "When the first man stands on the moon next month, *every American will stand taller* because of what he has done."[18]

Alas, it is merely a cliché that politicians, like various advertisers, seek to make us feel "tall in the saddle." The important thing to observe is the way this particular trait fits into the constellation of our President's whole personality, and the way it may affect his decisions. When Vietnam policy, for example, is defended on the grounds that the United States must not act "like a pitiful, helpless giant," when we are afraid of being thought "impotent," then something additional is involved. At that point Nixon seems to be identifying himself and the country rather too closely, as when he says, "It is not our power but our will and character that are being tested tonight." Is this the "deep need to draw the line at what he [Nixon] called the intolerable" noticed by Max Frankel (for the full quote, see p. 168)?

A similar point: in the first two short paragraphs of Nixon's speech on Cambodia, the pronoun "I" is used six times. The speech as a whole is filled with "I have concluded," "I shall describe," "This is my decision," and other similar phrases. We also have "we will not be humiliated," "we will not be defeated," and the repetitive threat that if the enemy's attacks continue to "humiliate and defeat us," we shall react accordingly. All of this is placed in a context of "real crisis," in which we must not be found wanting. Whatever the military and political arguments for and against the Cambodian action, and the later judgment on its results, we cannot help but con-

**117**

clude that the crisis was a "crisis" for Nixon personally, as well as for the country, and that for him his ability to be strong and decisive was at stake.

Nixon's need, indeed compulsion, to be strong is closely connected with his fear of dependency; that is, the need to accept his own desire to be passive and dependent, to be given to and taken care of, as in the case of a helpless child. (The threat is that the source of supply may disappear; as the psychoanalyst Otto Fenichel puts it, "the fear that the external means of satisfaction might possibly fail to arrive. It is the 'fear over loss of love' or rather loss of help and protection.") Nixon's father provided the model. "I remember," Nixon tells us, "that my Dad sold half of the acre on which our house was located in order to pay medical bills. My Dad was an individual—he'd go to his grave before he took government help. This attitude of his gave us pride. Maybe it was false pride, but we had it."[19] In this recollection we again see how overdetermined was Nixon's OPA experience and his resulting "conversion." Wills captures the dynamics involved when he writes, "A man can be self-made only by himself. . . . Turning the job over to government is a confession that one *needs* government, a confession of weakness, an admission that *self*-government has failed."[20]

Discussing Nixon's refusal to ask help from Eisenhower or anyone else during the 1960 Presidential campaign, a White House aide explained, "You must start with a basic psychological fact—that Nixon is an introspective man. He just can't *ask* anybody for help. He could have had our help any time he wanted. . . . But Nixon couldn't bring himself to ask help of anybody."[21] The reality, of course, is that, asked for or not, Nixon was constantly *being* helped by others. For example, a 1958 strategy meeting was held in Key Biscayne, Florida, for Nixon and his advisors; their host, we are told, "was an undistinguished though wealthy Florida businessman, whose hospitality had been lavishly extended to Richard M. Nixon since his first prominence as a young Congressman in the late 1940s."[22] The "undistinguished" businessman is "Bebe" Rebozo, Nixon's great intimate, who also helped him build up his personal fortune. From 1953 on Nixon was also befriended by Elmer H. Bobst, former president of Hoffman-LaRoche, the large pharmaceutical producer, and more lately the moving force in Warner-Lambert Co. As Nixon's foster father, or "Uncle Elmer" as he became to the Nixon girls, Bobst showered affection and attention on his protégé. As Bobst reminisces, "through the offer of a political friend who had two houses nearby, the Nixon family used a house near me for four weeks that summer. . . . I got him honorary membership in my clubs, and arranged for golf lessons for him." Bobst, along with Donald Kendall, president of Pepsi-Cola Company, also arranged Nixon's entry, as head, into the law firm of Mudge, Rose (after the 1962 gubernatorial defeat); Bobst's firm, Warner-Lambert, was Nixon's first client in the firm, and Kendall's Pepsi-Cola his second.[23]

Needless to say, this is a commonplace and fairly innocent part of political life. People like to help a potentially successful political candidate (who can also help them, even if only in their sense of self-esteem). What is noteworthy is Nixon's strong feelings about, and fear of, dependency wishes. He cannot admit to himself some of his innermost desires. He must publicly and fervently reject any hint of passivity or dependency; he must appear solely as strong and independent, a man of lonely but forceful decisions. Alas, his ambivalent feelings break through in reality and in speeches; his denial of them only adds to the vague feeling of distrust that he induces in many people.

With his compulsive need for strength, Nixon also combines a noteworthy streak of compassion. He has, I believe, a real sympathy for the poor and deprived, as long as they are not being coddled or made "self-indulgent," and he sincerely backs the Family Assistance Plan. In his August 15, 1971 speech on his new economic policies, he sounded only the note of competitive strength. But with this established he could then add the following in his August 18 speech to the Knights of Columbus: "America became a great nation, a strong nation, a rich nation, because we have a competitive spirit. During the past quarter century . . . we often curbed our competitive spirit. But now the time has come to be ourselves again—still compassionate, still with a sense of responsibility toward others in the world, still fair, still ready to help those who need help—but also determined to show what we can do, and to compete with other nations without tying one hand behind our back." The next day in Springfield, Illinois, Nixon put it in a nutshell when he implicitly compared himself to Lincoln, who was "kind and compassionate and considerate on the one hand, and strong and competitive on the other."

Nixon's compassion spills over into private relations as well as public proposals. As many officials and reporters, generally to their own surprise, have discovered, Nixon is a considerate man. Jules Witcover, for example, was touched when, during the 1966 electoral campaign, Nixon ordered a plane held for him. Daniel Patrick Moynihan has insisted, "Let me say with absolute candor that I think he is the most civil man I have ever worked for. . . . [He, Nixon] really does have some sense of your own feelings."[24] Garry Wills points out how "he has an extraordinary empathy with despondent people. . . ."[25]

Part of this may be the boy who grew up in a family touched by poverty, where one Fourth of July his family was the only one in the neighborhood too poor to afford firecrackers for its children,[26] and who can therefore sympathize with the needy. A large part, surely, is the example of his grandmother and mother taking care of others. The largest part, however, I believe, relates to Nixon's denial of his own needs, dependencies, and weaknesses. When he can do this successfully and feel strong, then he can "afford," in his psychic economy, to be compassionate. It never occurs to Nixon, who speaks of Americans as "ready to help those who need help," that America itself might be constantly being helped by other nations in various important ways. This would cut too close to the bone of his deepest feelings. A strong Nixon can give; he cannot take.

One way of trying to understand this trait a bit more clearly is to introduce the concept of orality. Freud first worked out the notion of an oral stage in an infant's development, and Erik Erikson has brilliantly expanded the concept in terms of an individual's psychosocial development. Following Erikson, who builds on Freud, we can talk of oral modes of behavior. The infant first encounters the external world with his mouth. he nurses. In order to live he must "take in." If the mother is nervous, or milk is not sufficiently available, problems can arise. Normally, however, the child learns to "incorporate" and "retain," that is, not spit up, what the mother has to give. Gradually, as the child acquires teeth, he also learns to "bite"—the mother's breast (which can evoke a traumatic reaction on her part at times) and other objects. Eventually, weaning occurs, and the child may feel "deprived" of its ready source of nourishment and warmth.

Erikson extends these early childhood experiences to what he calls the "oral mode," which in later life may actually be detached from the oral zone itself. Thus, we speak of "biting" sarcasm. We call our lovers "good enough to eat." We say in anger, "You make me sick," meaning we cannot digest or accept what is being thrust at us. We "spit out" words in disgust. The oral mode, in short, plays out our patterns of incorporation, expectoration, taking, giving, and so forth.

How might this apply to Nixon? Although detailed data is not available, it seems worthwhile to notice a few points concerning his orality (a term I use in order to avoid the technical demands of talking about his "oral stage"). First, there is the odd fact that Nixon, whose mother loved to cook, has little interest in "good" food. It is commonplace knowledge that his favorite foods are such things as hamburgers and spaghetti (to celebrate the Republican gains in 1966, Nixon took his friends to El Morocco for a bowl of his favorite spaghetti). Mazo and Hess inform us that while Nixon's mother was in Arizona, taking care of Harold, the father, Richard, and the other boys "took turns preparing the meals—usually canned chili, spaghetti, pork and beans, soup, and at least half the menus consisted of either hamburgers or fried eggs. Odd as it may seem, I like all of those things,' Nixon admits. 'There were many mornings when I ate nothing for breakfast but a candy bar.' "27

It does seem odd, and the oddity is compounded when we learn that at college Nixon gave away his mother's carefully prepared pies (in the early days Hannah Nixon used to get up before dawn to bake pies for sale in the grocery store) and sandwiches to his friends.28 Why this abstinence from food that his mother prided herself on making? Had she either "stuffed" him too much in his early years or been an uncertain source of supplies, especially in the Arizona years. Nixon's feelings about dependency suggest the latter, although his habit of referring to what's on his "plate"—Wills reports as one of his favorite metaphors, "There is enough on the plate, don't add to it"29—must give us pause. Whatever the answer, there is little question that Nixon had a problem of sorts related to food. As a schoolmate recalls, before a football game the main course was always steak, and Nixon invariably was "too tensed up" to eat.

The orality factor also manifests itself in Nixon's crises. At the beginning he seems almost to feed on a crisis; he seems to become drunk on the very froth of political warfare. But then comes the reaction, and what appears to be a case of oral depletion (thus deepening and adding to our earlier analysis of the crisis as one of aggression). Nixon's images are basically "oral" images, relating to his "insides." Thus, we have seen him refer in the Hiss case to the "intense desire to act and speak decisively *which I had kept bottled up inside myself*" (my italics), and in the Eisenhower heart attack episode he spoke of "not know-ing how to act or not being able to act is what *tears your insides out.*" At the end he reiterates his feeling of being "drained . . . emotionally." (Psychosomatic illness, such as ulcers, would be compatible with such feelings.)

Orality is also Nixon's preferred mode of releasing aggres-sion. We spoke earlier of "biting" sarcasm. Speech can be a means of attacking others, and Nixon developed early his skills at debating. For a boy who never spoke back to his intemperate father, but who "talked" his way around him, debate and acting must have come as a great relief. In his oral aggression Nixon could both identify with his father, who also used to like to argue about everything, and, in a more subtle sense, finally talk back to him. In what appears to be his feeling of oral deple-tion, we seem to sense a fear of dependence, a feeling that nourishment (emotional as well as physical) is uncertain, or else too erratic—stuffed at one moment, and starving at an-other. The picture is by no means clear, but one thing is certain: orality is an important element in Nixon's character.

Just as Freud and Erikson speak of oral stages, zones, and modes, so they refer to anal stages, zones, and modes of de-velopment. (Needless to say, every individual will partake in some measure of both modes.) The anal deals primarily with modes of elimination or of retention, of control and of stubborn-ness. We shall use the term "anality" in this connection; we have already pointed out its presence in Nixon's reply to Eisen-hower. It remains, therefore, to say only a very few more words on this subject.

An initial observation is that Nixon is not alone in his anality. Others frequently use similar metaphors. One odd use, however, occurs in Nixon's combination of a genital metaphor and an anal one. In his disastrous speech to the press after his 1962 gubernatorial defeat, Nixon spoke of the reporters as giv-ing him the "shaft." Then, according to *Time,* Nixon turned to his assistant Klein and said, "I gave it to them right in the behind."[30] Somehow, for the man with the iron butt, this seems a particularly fitting expression!

In themselves trivial, Nixon's anal metaphors become more important if we see them as a clue leading to his intense need for control: control of himself, control of others, and control of the world around him. At its best control, rooted in the anal stage according to Freud, leads to autonomy, to control over oneself as a form of independence. At its worst it leads to over-control, to rigidity, to a constricting fear of "letting go." Nixon seems to exhibit both aspects of control. His "lonely decisions" suggest he has achieved a form of autonomy, whatever its practical political drawbacks. His notorious body rigidity, with his mechanical gestures, suggests a desperate need for control of himself, which in turn means compulsive control of his situation.*

Nixon is partly aware of his need for control. "I have a fetish about disciplining myself," he confessed.[31] Even his smile, which can be winning or radiant, is seldom allowed to show itself; it would be too much "letting go" for Nixon. In his overall political manner and style, Nixon, however, has made a virtue out of his intense personal need for control. As Wit-cover perceptively points out, "He was, without doubt, at his best on the formal platform . . . where he always was in con-trol, where he could ask himself the questions and then answer them, where he could provide the sense of intimacy he sought through the use of the political catechism he long ago mas-tered: 'You ask me, "Mr. Nixon, why do we have to reject appeasement?" And I tell you, we have to reject appeasement because peace at any price is always a down payment on a bigger war.' "[32] In short, gaining control over himself, Nixon

---

* In 1968, Theodore White perceived a "new Nixon" in this regard: "His hands still moved as he spoke, but the fingers spread gracefully, not punchily or sharply as they used to." (White, *Making of President, 1968,* p. 533.)

then turns that self-control into control over his audience. It is an impressive performance.

What we have been discussing up to now may be thought of as the psychological banalities of Nixon's character. More important is what he has done with them. No man reaches his position without a good deal of ability, and Nixon starts with strong cognitive powers: he is quick, shrewd, and possessed of a good memory. Moreover, he has turned his problems and weaknesses into challenges and strengths. Racked by indecision, he has learned how to plan and contrive ahead of time. Faced with the constant need to test himself, he has shown real courage on a number of occasions. His aggressive projections are in tune with those of many of his fellow Americans. His quiet fundamentalism accords with the uses of religion of a large segment of the American people. His acting is so good that he has become his roles.

Since 1962 he has matured, coming to grips with his fear of failure and his death wishes toward the father figure, Eisenhower. The nadir for Nixon was the gubernatorial defeat of 1962. After that, he returned to success via his first ambition: to be a big Eastern corporation lawyer. With an income of $200,000 a year and substantial holdings in Florida land (as advised by Rebozo), Nixon could stand "taller." When he finally won the Presidency in 1968, he won it on his own, owing nothing to Eisenhower. By this time, too, Nixon had solidified his method of meeting "crises." His control of impulse, his planning and deliberation were greater than ever.

With these statements in mind, when I first began my analysis of Nixon, I made some provisional estimates about his future behavior. In fairness to the reader, let me repeat some of these tentative "predictions" so that he can judge their validity before we enter upon a fuller discussion of Nixon's actual performance as President. At the time I wrote as follows: "The memory of Shakespeare's Henry IV must give us pause, as we seek to predict the behavior not of Kings, but of Presidents as they reach their new office. Prince Henry, as King Henry IV, confounded Falstaff and all his former companions by his totally changed behavior. Will Nixon be another Henry IV, a 'new' Nixon?"

I did not think so at the time. Indeed, I thought that Nixon's policy as President would correspond closely to the aspects of his personality mentioned earlier. In line with this, and his character as a pragmatic and expedient politician, I believed that the demands of the office, and of political necessity, would largely determine his actions. Walter Lippmann had written persuasively that the actual situation of the United States demands a "deflationary" policy: to deflate the economy, reduce political promises, and cut down our overseas commitments (for example, Vietnam). As Lippmann concluded, "The role of the deflator is never glamorous. Has there ever been a 'charismatic' deflator?" At this point I wrote, "Nixon, surely, is not charismatic. Perhaps, as Lippmann suggests, it is Nixon's destiny to have his 'pragmatic' character exactly fit the needs of his time and the mood of the American people." Then I continued: "What of the needs and aspirations of America and its people that lie outside the 'deflationary' situation? These, unfortunately for Nixon, may grow larger. The problems of blacks, of youth, of possible recession and uncontrollable inflation, of wars and commitments cannot easily be collapsed. Will Nixon's sort of noncharismatic leadership succeed in such circumstances, or might he tend to lose his 'cool'? I confess to a haunting sense of doubt as to Nixon's ability to rise to such challenges.

"If Lippmann is right, then Nixon will not be severely 'tested.' In that case we need only be on the lookout for certain fundamental features of Nixon's character, especially his 'pragmatism,' continuously to assert themselves. The John Knowles controversy [head of Massachusetts General Hospital, Knowles was the choice of Finch, then Secretary of HEW,

for the top health position in government; after a long indecisive period, Nixon withdrew his initial support for the
appointment] suggests that he will continue to agonize over
decisions, but will eventually make them, often with a good
sense of timing. At requisite moments he will *create* crises, as
a means of testing himself and assuring himself greater public
support. I am positive that he will continue to make irrecon-
cilable statements, such as promising not to embroil America
in future Vietnams at the same time as he pledges similar
assistance to Thailand. He will do this because, in the presence
of any given audience, Nixon believes implicitly in the 'lines'
he is uttering. I emphasize that he is an 'actor,' not an 'ideo-
logue.' "

How does this "analysis" stand up today? The reader must
judge for himself. My task now is to examine Nixon's behavior
since 1968 in actual "crises," to take up anew, and more
systematically, the evidence for a "changed" Nixon, and to
summarize these findings as they appear in 1972. Then, the
reader can judge for himself how valid my total analysis is
and how much it helps deepen his understanding of the meaning and significance of Nixon's behavior.


## The Haynsworth-Carswell Nomination

The Haynsworth-Carswell crisis, for it was really one event,
must be our first case study. Almost all observers agree that
it was extraordinarily revealing of Nixon's character. Typical
is Tom Wicker's comment at the time, "It has certainly revealed the man,"[33] or Richard Harris' observation that "of
all the actions that President Richard Nixon took during his
first two years in office, probably none more clearly revealed the
character of his Presidency."[34]

What was revealed? On the surface political level Nixon

revealed himself as a man who, while talking of "bringing us together," tried to pit section against section in the country. He was willing to do this, it seems, in order to pay his debt to Southern supporters, such as Strom Thurmond, and to ensure the continuing success of his Southern Strategy. Besides, the proposed appointments were congenial to Nixon because they fitted his strict constructionist interpretation of the Constitution.

Now, paying political debts, securing future supporters, and wanting strict constructionists on the court are not in themselves heinous intentions. What made the proposed appointment a *cause célèbre* was Nixon's vehement, personal involvement in them. The first thing to notice is how poor a performance this was for Nixon, a lawyer. (An increasingly recurrent trait, one may observe, as in his "slip" about the Charles Manson case—calling him guilty before the trial verdict was given—and in his intervention in the Calley case, although the latter can be "explained away" as an obviously political move.) When in 1966 Nixon pleaded his first case before the Supreme Court, he informed Chief Justice Earl Warren that "he had prepared for the case by reviewing sixty years of New York decisions in the area of invasion of privacy [the particular issue involved]."[35] Nixon's triumphant performance proved it. Now, in his first nomination to the Supreme Court, surely a more important case, we are told that Nixon himself had never met Haynsworth and that his Attorney General, John Mitchell, had never even heard of the Haynsworth legal firm. The dossier prepared on Haynsworth, as we all know, seems to have reflected a similar ignorance of the man's record.

The Senate's rejection of Haynsworth, because of the man's insensitivity to potential conflicts of interest, was obviously not pleasant medicine for any President to have to take. It clearly exposed a Presidential blunder, though a forgiveable one. But Nixon's overreaction made a serious case out of the matter, inadvertently revealing his "real" character. As is his pattern,

Nixon refused to admit that he might have been in error. The best defense, as always, was offense, and Nixon passed to the offensive, spending nights "rereading Congressional records of the struggles over the similarly controversial nominations of Louis Brandeis and Charles Evans Hughes."[36] There is a certain compulsiveness here: Nixon is returning to his "heroes" of college days, in a desperately misplaced analogy (Brandeis, like Haynsworth, came from the South—Louisville—but there the analogy ends), and boning up for the case, as he had in his 1966 appearance before the Supreme Court, only this time it was too late.

What the Brandeis-Hughes reading does tell us, however, is that Nixon was personally overinvolved in this case. The second nomination of G. Harrold Carswell on January 19, 1970, makes this point blatantly. Reviewing the nomination, William V. Shannon summed it up well: "It was a deliberate, provocative, crude, and inexcusable act of political *aggression* against the President's opponents, against the Senate, and against the Supreme Court itself."[37] Like another of his heroes, Woodrow Wilson, before him, Nixon seemed to be telling the Senate it must now "take its medicine."

Did Nixon *want* the Senate to reject his second appointment as well? Was he trying to prove that he had not made a mistake the first time, but that a vicious Senate, prejudiced against the South, was solely responsible? Carswell's nomination, coming after Haynsworth, certainly seems to be a "Heads, I win, Tails you lose" proposition: Carswell was so clearly unfit for the Supreme Court that confirmation would have meant outright surrender to Nixon's "aggression," yet rejection, at least in Nixon's eyes, provided proof of his self-serving thesis.

A close reading of Nixon's statement of August 9, 1970, on his Supreme Court choices shows mammoth projection at work. The text itself seems to have been decided upon solely with the advice of Attorney General Mitchell—a way for Nixon to show that he had not lost faith in his "strong" man—and

H. R. Haldeman, during a short cruise on board the Presidential yacht. The way in which the decision was made prompted one reporter, Robert B. Semple, Jr., to observe that "the President had not altered his patterns of retreating from the White House for more private surroundings in advance of major decisions. This was also his practice before the Inaugural Address, the November 3rd speech on Vietnam and his long statement on desegregation two weeks ago."[38] In his "lonely decision" Nixon identified himself closely, it appears, with his nominees. "Judges Carswell and Haynsworth," he declared, "have endured with admirable dignity vicious assaults on their intelligence, their honesty and their character." Do we not hear echoes here of the Nixon who saw himself "smeared" in the 1940s and 1950s and constantly assaulted by a vicious press?

"But," Nixon continued, "when all the hypocrisy is stripped away, the real issue was their philosophy of strict construction of the Constitution—*a philosophy that I share* (my italics)—and the fact that they had the misfortune of being born in the South." Having thus distorted the motives of his opponents, Nixon went on in spoiled child fashion, his statement serving also as a clever form of the self-fulfilling prophecy: "My next nominee will be from outside the South and he will fulfill the criteria of strict constructionist with judicial experience. . . ." Repeating his basic point—which I am identifying as a form of projection—Nixon declared, "I will not nominate another southerner and let him be subjected to the kind of malicious character assassination accorded both Judges Haynsworth and Carswell." He then concluded with an open threat. "I understand the bitter feelings of millions of Americans who live in the South . . . they have my assurance that the day will come when men like Judges Carswell and Haynsworth can and will sit on the high court."

Nixon, in short, will be vindicated and will emerge victorious. Meanwhile, he had lost and lost badly. As in 1962 failure for

130

Nixon seems to be an almost intolerable emotion, dealt with by verbal aggression that seeks to deny his own role in that failure and to accuse his opponents of malicious and unfair behavior. It is not I, he seems to be saying, who might be at fault, but only those "others." Moreover, one's own aggressive and nasty impulses can be imputed to the "others" as well. In the Haynsworth-Carswell case, then, the pattern of projection still runs strong in Nixon, even as President.

## The Cambodian Episode

The Carswell failure, and, in a sense, humiliation, seems to have triggered a train of decisions by Nixon in which his personal feelings seem to have been unusually involved. His speech on Carswell was given on April 9, 1970. On April 20 he revealed his plans to withdraw 150,000 troops from Vietnam. Although during the 1968 campaign he had made dovish-sounding statements on Vietnam, Nixon had been a consistent hard-liner, insisting that all that was involved was aggression by the communist North, as part of the world-wide communist conspiracy. In hyperbolic terms he insisted that the loss of "freedom" there meant the loss of freedom everywhere in the world. Nixon seemed to set up a "moral domino" theory, with one humiliating defeat setting off a chain of further humiliations, ending only in total failure and loss of freedom.

Yet in his campaign Nixon had also vowed to end the war. If it couldn't actually be won as a war, then at least Nixon could claim that he would "win the peace." Vietnamization and the gradual withdrawal of American troops was the strategy, not negotiation with the enemy and an acceptance of one's defeat (for such it is). The April 20 troop withdrawal was announced in this context.

Then, on April 27, Nixon decided to move into Cambodia,

131

presumably to protect the troops remaining in Vietnam. Everybody seems to have been surprised by Nixon's decision, according to James Reston, except the enemy. As Reston put it, Nixon's action increased anxiety and division; even his own supporters felt that it had been reached with undue haste and carried out by deception. To allay the anxiety and to explain his actions, Nixon gave his now famous speech of April 30, 1970. We have already called attention to its repeated use of the "I" form—to show decisiveness—and its constant concern lest America be seen as humiliated, defeated, a pitiful helpless giant. In this crisis "our" character was being tested—there is no mention of the objective situation—and our task is not to be found wanting. Characteristically, Nixon justifies his aggressive actions by insisting that it is only the North Vietnamese who have violated the neutrality of Cambodia, and that his actions do not constitute an invasion.

On the very next day, May 1, Nixon, in some remarks to a group of Pentagon employees who greeted him as he arrived for a briefing on the United States military operation in Cambodia, referred to his radical student opponents as "bums," contrasting them with the "kids" doing their duty and standing "tall." As we have suggested, aggressive feelings are all right if directed against "bums." Coming shortly after the Carswell episode—a real defeat—Nixon's incursion into Cambodia and attack on his "peacenik" critics must have been very satisfying emotionally.

The unexpected tragedy at Kent State obviously shook the President. His "aggression," for once, it seems, had had directly visible results beyond the verbal. Four students—alas, students, but not apparently "bums"—lay dead as a consequence of the chain of events unleashed by Nixon's "decision." As a basically peaceful man (for so I believe Nixon to be), he was—I am convinced—deeply affected in his own psyche by these deaths. No other explanation can make much sense out of his extraordinary predawn visit of May 9 to the Lincoln Memorial and his chat there with the antiwar students.

Unable to sleep, Nixon left the White House, accompanied only by his long-time valet, Manolo Sanchez, and the inevitable Secret Servicemen, but otherwise catching his staff unawares. The choice of the Lincoln Memorial seems overdetermined: Lincoln was a hero for Nixon, going back to his grandmother's days (a portrait of Lincoln had hung over Nixon's bed as a young boy); Lincoln had sought to "win the peace" and hold the nation together, actions specifically compared to his own by Nixon as early as a 1960 speech; and Lincoln, too, if I remember rightly, had taken a midnight walk and stopped to talk with an unknown soldier and to explain why the soldier and his buddies might have to die.

In the *New York Times* account we are told that Nixon's encounter with thirty to fifty students "appears to have been more monologue than dialogue," ending with an appeal to the students "to try to understand what we are doing."[39] After his return to the White House, Nixon related to Garnett D. Horner, correspondent for the *Washington Star,* some of what he had said. "On the war thing," Nixon reported, "I said [to the students] I know you think we are a bunch of so and sos— I used a stronger word to them [that is, bastards]. I know how you feel—you want to get the war over." Then Nixon told them how in 1939 he had had the wrong perspective on Chamberlain and Churchill. After his justification of his actions, which appears to have been a justification to himself as well, Nixon, we are informed, went to breakfast at the Mayflower Hotel where he had "corned beef hash with an egg on it." (One of the awful things about being President is that even one's breakfast is reported on; while grist for the psychohistorical mill, one cannot help being a little sorry for the continuous invasion of the man's privacy.) Mr. Nixon, the article concludes, told his aid, Mr. Ziegler, that it was his first corned beef hash with poached egg in five years. After the catharsis, an acceptable short regression in orality!

The account by some of the students of what transpired is bound to be suspect, partly because of their *parti pris* and partly because of the sensational nature of their comments, but it cannot be completely put aside. All seemed to agree that they had seen a more human Nixon than they had expected. Nicholas Stark, for example, commented that "through talking he changed my opinion—not on the issues—but of him as a human being". But most found that revelation frightening. "The vibrations in the air were scary," said Ronnie Kemper, the nineteen-year-old president of the sophomore class at Syracuse University. "You had an impulse to reach out and touch him to see if he was real." "We walked away hoping it was an actor doing a super goof," recalled Joan Pelletier, city editor of the Syracuse student newspaper. Another student, Dan Maring of Alfred, observed, "He was tired . . . he looked awfully tired and depressed . . . he looked at the floor a lot." Lynn Schatzkin, also from Syracuse, found his physical appearance upsetting. "His hands were in his pockets; he didn't look at any one in the eyes; he was mumbling; when people asked him to speak up he would boom one word and no more. As far as sentence structure [is concerned] there was none." Miss Pelletier recalled, "He looked like he had a mask on. He was wearing pancake make-up. He looked scared and nervous like he was in a fog. His eyes were glassy."[40]

Allowing for hyperbole in these descriptions, we still discern a Nixon deeply disturbed, tired, and apparently in a state of depression. In this bizarre episode we seem to see a reactivation, brought on by the four Kent State deaths, of Nixon's death anxieties, which we have described earlier. One of Nixon's reported comments was "I'm a devout Quaker. I'm against killing as much as you are and I want to bring the boys home." This *is* a very human person speaking, not just a cool, detached

President, making grand policy. As Robert Semple noted, Nixon had been under exceptional strain since the Cambodian operation, enjoying few restful nights since that decision and the consequent events culminating in Kent State. I am suggesting that the deeper roots of that strain go back to the Haynsworth-Carswell case, and beyond that, to Nixon's earliest years. As in music one can hear the harmonies surrounding even a single note that is struck.

Nixon, however, weathered this personal, as well as political, crisis, and pulled himself together; control reasserted itself. I would speculate that the months of April–May 1970 imposed the greatest strain on Nixon's psyche since 1962. It is a tribute to his "strength of character" and his dogged perseverance that he suffered merely a depression and not a breakdown, though the latter may have been close. Once in control of himself again, however, Nixon reaffirmed his game plan. He refused to give way to his critics on Vietnam and continued on the path he had outlined in his November 3, 1969 speech. He pursued his Southern Strategy and law and order appeals in the congressional election campaign, culminating in the notorious San Jose episode (with its deliberate replay of Caracas). As if to reaffirm the rightness of Cambodia, he launched a Laotian operation as well (admittedly, a failure).

Nixon, it appears, had not changed. Shaken by Kent State, which reactivated and reawakened all sorts of feelings, Nixon had regained his composure and control. Only failure of his law and order campaign of 1970 "changed" Nixon, in my opinion. At this point his basic pragmatism reasserted itself. Again, he began to take the "high" road and to "bring us together" anew. More recently, he has moved boldly and decisively on his China policy; but, as I shall suggest shortly, that, too, is really an "old," not a "new" Nixon at work. The complete change-about on wage and price control is, again, the masking of a "failure" by a "decisive" offensive.

## The New Economic Policy

The dramatic reversal on August 15, 1971, of Nixon's own economic policy can be viewed as another example of his crisis behavior. Under attack not only by his enemies but by his friends for not taking action on the unemployment and inflation front, Nixon, after months and months of asserting he would not impose wage-price controls, suddenly changed his mind. Two things are noteworthy. First, Nixon never admitted that he had been in error, that is, that his economic policies had not been working. Second, he made an unexpected and decisive conversion, passing to the offensive and claiming a bold new economic policy (which it is). Discussing his proposed action, Nixon made a strong case: "We are going to take that action, not timidly, not half-heartedly, not in piecemeal fashion. We are going to move forward to the new prosperity without war as befits a great people—all together, ["bring us together"?] and along a broad front." Vigor and decisiveness mark his entire text. Moreover, Nixon pre-empts the Vietnam war issue by assuming in his first few sentences that *that* war is won— we have won the peace—and now we must pass on to the problems of "prosperity without war." Thus, Nixon is really advancing victoriously on two fronts, fitting his economic offensive neatly into his general dedication to peace.

The next thing to note is that Nixon has not repudiated the rhetoric and psychological commitment of his OPA experience, although he has, in fact, sold out the substance. He insists the freeze is voluntary (though backed by government coercion). "While the wage-price freeze will be backed by government sanction if necessary," Nixon declared, "it will not be accompanied by the establishment of a huge price-control bureaucracy." At no point, however, has he made it clear how government coercion could, in fact, be brought to bear without bureaucratic intervention. Thus, for many observers, a reality gap remains.

Regarding the problem of "protecting" the dollar abroad (and military images abound in Nixon's prosperity with peace presentation), Nixon places all the blame not on ourselves (for example, on our vast military expenditures abroad) but on the "others." They must "bear their fair share of the burden of defending freedom around the world." While couched in "freedom" rhetoric, this is basically a fair point. But when Nixon passes over to an attack on the "international speculators," surely the effect not the cause of the problem, we sense personal projection at work again. "I am determined," Nixon declares firmly, "that the American dollar must never again be a hostage in the hands of the international speculators." Shades of the prisoners of war, as hostages in the hands of the North Vietnamese! Nixon's next accusation also sounds familiar to us at this point in our book. "Because they thrive on crisis, they [the speculators] help to create them [sic]."

One final quotation encapsulates much of the Nixon we have discussed. A "nation," Nixon says, "like a person, has to have a certain inner drive in order to succeed. In economic affairs, that inner drive is called the competitive spirit. Every action I have taken tonight is designed to nurture and stimulate that competitive spirit, to help us snap out of that self-doubt and self-disparagement that saps our energy and erodes our confidence in ourselves. . . . We welcome this competition, because America is at her greatest when she is called on to compete. And no nation has anything to fear from our competition, because we lead our competitors on to new heights for their own people."

As is clear, we have not sought to analyze Nixon's New Economic Policy (reminiscent of Lenin's NEP?) in economic terms. Nor have we alluded to its obvious political functions, such as depriving his critics of their issue, thus preparing the way for the 1972 election. Instead, our inquiry has focused on the personal aspect of the action and speech. We have tried to analyze the New Economic Policy as a "crisis" for Nixon, partly of his own making. Seen in this light, it is sometimes difficult to know where the needs of Nixon and the United States begin and end. His crisis is also America's crisis. He mirrors the polity and its moods of confidence and self-doubt. Nixon's "strength with compassion" touches a deep chord, it seems, in his fellow countrymen. So do his fighting images. In short, person and policy, for good or for bad, seem inextricably mixed.

## The New China Policy

In the light of our general analysis so far, we ought to say a word about Nixon's recent decision to go to Peking. Though not a "crisis" per se, it falls within the general category of crisis decisions. First, it raises the question whether all of Nixon's old suspicions and projections about communism have disappeared. Have his feelings about the international conspiracy of communism changed? Such a reading would ignore all the evidence so far cited and fly in the face of our fundamental view of Nixon as an extraordinarily ambivalent man. Nixon, I suggest, still projects his personal unacceptable feelings onto an external enemy, in this case, communism. But he is also a pragmatist; of crucial importance, he also sincerely believes in working for peace. Only those who have not paid attention to Nixon's own words and character would be surprised at his so-called new China policy.

The basic context for Nixon's foreign policy *is* his dedication to peace. We have already seen parts of this psychological disposition in our discussion of his relations with Dr. Hutschnecker. It emerges in Nixon's support of Wendell Willkie and in his own declaration that he is a "whole-worlder." The roots of this conviction lie deep in the Nixon family, or rather in the women of his family. I believe we catch the real flavor of Nixon's feelings on the matter in an unusually candid statement he made to Walter Cronkite back in 1960. I quote at length:

Well, my major interest ever since I came to Washington, and long before that has been in the field of foreign policy and of foreign affairs. Now this does not mean that I haven't an interest in domestic affairs, as well, and haven't participated in many activities involving domestic issues. But, the reason that, to me the overriding issue of our times is foreign affairs, is where it comes right out of my whole background. I indicated, for example, that my mother is a Quaker, she is a very good one. I am not as good. But, from the time that I can remember, I know that she and my grandmother, her mother who lived to be 93, used to talk about their "concern," which is a Quaker way of expressing it, for building a better life not only for people in this country but for people everywhere. This humanitarian approach to the problems of the world, an approach, incidentally, which they have, my mother and my grandmother, more in their character than I have, but which I certainly have acquired from them to an extent; this is something that I think has affected my whole attitude toward public service generally.[11]

Nixon then concludes, "And, as I see the responsibilities for the next President . . . his major role will be to attempt to make a contribution toward building a world peace, with freedom for all people." At this point I am prepared to believe Nixon when he says he has "an obsession on this point."[42]

However, at this point, Nixon's other "obsessions" swing into action. For example, a few weeks before the interview with Cronkite, Nixon was on a Jack Paar show, where he said, "What happens any place in the world affects our freedom, and it might affect the peace of the world."[43] Here we have echoes of Nixon's hyperbolic identification of *his* crises with world crises, only in reverse (and I say this without ignoring the reality factor in Nixon's statement). Nixon proceeds: "I think that we can have peace. I think that we can keep our own freedom, and I think that we can win the struggle against slavery and for freedom throughout the world. . . ."[44] Again, the useful division into all good and all bad, all black and all white, slavery and freedom, aggressor and peace-loving one-worlder.

Nixon, like so many of his generation, is a consistent cold war warrior. Cognitively, he remembers that appeasement led to World War II. As he recalls telling the protesting students in his predawn visit to the Lincoln Memorial, ". . . I know it is awfully hard to keep this in perspective. I told them that in 1938 I thought Neville Chamberlain was the greatest man living and Winston Churchill was a madman. It was not until years later that I realized Neville Chamberlain was a good man but Winston Churchill was right."[45]

This cognitive knowledge fits perfectly with Nixon's personal feelings about being strong. As he told Cronkite, "I think the way . . . to have peace is to be strong and be prepared to resist those who threaten peace."[46] It also fits with his fierce conviction about competitiveness: peace is something that must be "won." As he said about the Vietnam war: "It is essential that we end this war, and end it quickly, but . . . in such a way that we win the peace."[47] For Nixon the great danger is that he and America will go "soft," will appear "impotent," will allow themselves to be "humiliated." As we pointed out once before, it never seems to occur to Nixon that he or America might use strength for "aggressive" purposes, even though cognitively he might recognize that Americans "conquered" this continent and the Indians on it, brought in millions of slaves, fought a war for territory against Mexico, and so forth.

In this context of mixed and ambivalent feelings we must place Nixon's changing policy vis-à-vis Communist China. First, there are good political (that is, electoral) reasons for his dramatic decision to go to Peking. It is *dramatic* and appears to be the action of a *decisive* man. Nixon must have recalled that his trip to Russia and his debate with Khrushchev had immediately lifted his standing in the polls from behind Rockefeller to frontrunner. "Statesmanship," like "crises," rallies people to a leader. His Peking plan also recalls Eisenhower's willingness to go to Russia (and Nixon, we have seen, though ambivalent about Ike, also admired him tremendously). Next, there are good pragmatic reasons for the move toward Red China, much as it has dumbfounded Nixon's right-wing supporters. It exerts pressure on the Soviet Union (the one rationale acceptable to Nixon's right wing). And it accords with developments in the United Nations, where the United States has not been able to keep Mainland China from replacing Taiwan. Nixon, as a shrewd poker player, knows when to cut his losses.

Lastly, the new China policy fits, cognitively and emotionally, with Nixon's "obsession" with peace. For anyone who has read Theodore White's account of the 1968 campaign, Nixon's position should not have come as a surprise. "We talked of guerrillas, terrorists, and insurrectionary warfare," White recounts, "and then he [Nixon] said that if he were elected President the very first thing he'd do would be to try to get in touch with Red China. There had to be an understanding with Red China. In ten or fifteen years it would be impossible to run the world if Red China weren't part of it."[48] In his acceptance speech Nixon reiterated his position: "To the leaders of the Communist world we say, after an era of confrontations, the time has come for an era of negotiations . . . we extend the hand of friendship to all people. To the Russian people. *To the Chinese people.* To all people in the world."[49]

Nixon, as a "strong" man, operating from strength, could negotiate with other "strong" men; in fact, he admired them. Only those who have come to doubt anything said by "Tricky Dicky" would doubt his real, though ambivalent, feelings about peace. I cite one last paragraph by White of Nixon's views:

. . . if you were looking ahead as far as three or four years, there was the China problem—which was why Japan was developing a new sense of urgency, he felt. That's why it was important to have

141

the Asian nations develop their own "collective security." The Asians weren't quite ready for that yet; he meant, he explained, they couldn't yet defend their own internal security; only when China realized that she couldn't overthrow all other Asian nations would the way be open for an eventual dialogue with the Chinese—just as the dialogue with the Soviet Union had begun only after the Soviets had realized that the Europeans were strong enough to protect themselves. He was looking forward to starting the dialogue with China—but that would come only with an Asia strong enough to stand beside us politically, economically, internally, when the Chinese sensed that their own best interests would be served best by concentrating on their own internal problems.[50]

In statements such as this, and in his decision to go to Peking, we can see Nixon's ambivalences at work. His aggressive projections pull him one way; his mother, a "strong woman," dedicated to peace, pulls him another way. Logically, Nixon's erratic and ambivalent feelings lead him into seemingly incomprehensible positions. *Psycho*logically, however, we can see that there is indeed method to what occasionally looks like madness. Nixon's decision to visit Peking is a sterling example of that behavior pattern.

## A New Nixon?

Implicit in my analysis of Nixon's most recent "crises"—the Haynsworth-Carswell affair, Cambodia and Kent State, the New Economic Policy, the Peking decision—is my belief in a deep consistency to Nixon's pattern of behavior. Nixon is a man torn between his mother's dislike of warfare and his father's sharp competitiveness; thus, he is extremely ambivalent about his aggressive impulses and tends to deal with them by projection onto others. He is a man haunted by his father's "failure" and driven to avoid that failure for himself and to redeem it for his parent. He compensates for lack of native abilities, where this is the case, by enormous hard work and persistence. He is wracked by indecision and by the question of his own courage, especially in a crisis. He has had a serious problem with death wishes and anxiety in relation to his brothers, Eisenhower, and himself. He is an "actor" in the theatrical sense and releases himself verbally in debates. He is a fundamentalist in religion, with a passive acceptance of authority. He projects unacceptable impulses onto others. He identifies his personal interest with the national interest. He exalts strength and fears passivity. And so on and on.

With these patterns of behavior clearly in mind, we can now repeat our earlier questions. Has the man grown, or if not grown, has he at least changed? Before we seek to offer answers to these questions, we must briefly re-examine how others have handled this issue.

In his *The Making of the President, 1968,* Theodore White, makes an impressive case for a changed Nixon. "America," he writes, "had known many Richard Nixons. . . . What it had not yet perceived was the man . . . the character changed by learning and experience. Thus the story of Richard M. Nixon must move through this book on two tracks—the technical planning of a modern campaign in America, and the movement of the man in spirit from disaster to triumph, *seeking his own identity.*"[51] White concludes that the result is a changed Nixon, one who has grown as a man, as well as a leader.

In my view White has taken superficial changes for fundamental shifts. Richard Nixon has, in fact, remained true to himself, as a deeper analysis of his behavior patterns demonstrates. He has not changed in any fundamental sense. Nixon himself in 1960 took the same position. In his interview with Walter Cronkite he insisted that "many of those who discover the new Nixon may not know the old one, but seriously, may I say this: we all change."[52] By change, however, Nixon indicated he meant learning from eight years of experience under President Eisenhower. "I have learned a lot," he continued, "and it is very possible that I certainly do *convey a different impression* [my italics] than I did previously, because if I hadn't learned, I wouldn't amount to too much. So, I will concede that I have changed, and I hope for the better." Again, in 1966 Nixon declared, "There's been no significant change. People go through that psychological bit nowadays. They think they should always be reevaluating themselves. I fight the battles as they come along. That sort of juvenile self-analysis is something I've never done."[53] In 1968 he was more laconic about the so-called new Nixon. At his opening press conference in New Hampshire, he declared, "I believe I am better qualified to handle the great problems of the Presidency than I was in 1960. . . ."[54]

Jules Witcover, in his fine and detailed *The Resurrection of Richard Nixon,* suggests that the new Nixon was a man whose outward changes corresponded with the political need, after the Goldwater debacle of 1964, to project a "centrist" image, and thus to reunite his party. As both White and Witcover abundantly illustrate there is little question that the new Nixon was at one and the same time both a "looser" man—he could laugh at himself now—and a more "controlled" man, restraining his outbursts of irritability. Witcover's personal interview with Nixon in 1966 offers an extraordinary self-appraisal, which, as Witcover writes, was "either pure revelation or one of the great put-ons of the year." "I'm known as an activist and an organizer," Nixon said in the interview. Then he added rather proudly, "but some have said I'm sort of an egghead in the Republican party." He confessed to a fascinating daydream: "If I had my druthers, I'd like to write two or three books a year, go to one of the fine schools—Oxford, for instance—just teach, read and write." There followed a surprising, though illuminating comparison: "In order to make a decision, an individual should sit on his *rear end* and dig into the books. Very few executives do it. They listen to this side and that, but they don't go to the sources. In this respect, I'm like

144

Stevenson. . . . He was an intellectual and he needed time to contemplate."[55] Nixon's conclusion is equally interesting: "One thing I have to be is always be myself."[56]

I am inclined to believe Nixon in this last view, though perhaps with a different gloss from the one he intended. Hannah Nixon, when asked before 1960 about a new Nixon, replied, "No, he has always been exactly the same. I never knew a person to change so little. From the time he was first able to understand the world around him until now, he has reacted the same way to the same situations."[57] I join with this friendly critic. Nixon *has* always been himself, and that self has been steady and consistent throughout his life. Introspective, and almost analytic at times, he *has,* I believe, tried to understand himself, in the sense of recognizing his basic traits and seeking to guard against their hurting him politically. He has not, I believe, tried to change any of his traits, in the sense of going beyond them.

Much of that "self" and many of these traits are, I would concede, admirable. Persistence and hard work are virtues when rightly used. Such traits have allowed Nixon to change, in the sense of mastering his weaknesses and exercising greater and greater control over himself, even if not to grow spiritually. The various new Nixons attest to his ability to learn politically. I am also convinced of his sincere desire for peace and of his compassion for the needy. Many of his specific policies and programs are laudable. There is much to applaud in the thirty-seventh President of the United States.

Our concern, however, has been centered not so much on Nixon the external politician, as on the deeper aspects of the man as well as the President. Because we are interested in psychohistory, we are necessarily concerned with the correspondence of these aspects of Nixon's personality with those of Americans in general. For him and for us the subjective feelings often badly compromise and undercut the public policies. Thus, Nixon's dedication to peace has a corresponding element in powerful aggressive impulses and a tremendous competitive drive to win, and avoid any semblance of "defeat." The compassion for the needy finds a companion in the desperate need always to feel strong and to reject feelings of passivity and dependency.

In this book we have tried to illuminate those subjective feelings. If I had to sum up the outstanding personality traits of Richard Nixon, I would emphasize three. The first is his almost unique absorption of self in his role. For Nixon, though he does not recognize it, to always "be myself" is always to be the particular role in which he finds himself. Nixon *is* his role, as I have tried to show earlier. The second outstanding trait is Nixon's ambivalence. Ambivalence, of course, is in all of us. Yet as a scholar I have never dealt with a public figure as ambivalent as Nixon. The third trait, which is closely related to his ambivalence, is denial. Nixon uses mammoth denial as a defense against unacceptable impulses and feelings. He simply refuses, for example, to accept his aggressive intent, constantly saying things like, "I don't say this bitterly," when it is clear to everyone else that he *is* bitter (what's wrong with being bitter sometimes?).

These three traits together—role identification, ambivalence, and denial—have made Nixon one of the most difficult political figures to analyze. They add to what earlier I called his opaqueness and leave us with a feeling of constant uncertainty as to the nature of the "real" Nixon. They are also at the heart of the distrust so frequently felt about Nixon. Garry Wills catches a part of this picture when he compares Nixon to Uriah Heep in Dickens' *David Copperfield*. "This," he maintains, "explains the vague dislike for Nixon that many experience. It is not caused by any one thing he has done or omitted, but by an oppressive moralism and air of apology."[58] In my terms it is role ambiguity, ambivalence, and denial that necessarily must leave us uneasy about the real Richard Nixon.

There is one other important element in our vague feeling of unease about Nixon, an element that, moreover, corresponds significantly to the inner nature of many other Americans and to crucial aspects of this country's policy at home and abroad. We see this illustrated in Nixon's pervasive belief in his own goodness and morality. Un-selfconsciously, he quotes in *Six Crises* the faith in him expressed by Whittaker Chambers. "Almost from the day we met (think, it is already 12 years ago)," Chambers wrote to him, "I sensed in you some quality, deep-going, difficult to identify in the world's glib way, but good, and meaningful for you and multitudes of others."[59] This is the same Nixon who seems always to *act* in an amoral way, and who constantly asserts, for example, that "American foreign policy must always be directed by the security interests of the United States and not by some vague concept of 'world public opinion.'"[60] Granted that there is some truth to this latter remark, one must question whether "world public opinion," or informed domestic opinion, does not point to a morality, or immorality, that can lie hidden in a nation's, or an individual's, pursuit of power (under the name of protection and self-defense), and that also should be taken into account in formulating policy.

In short, if we have difficulty discovering the "real" Nixon, I believe that our President has even greater difficulty. Socrates counsels that "know thyself" is the right adage for a successful philosopher. Should a politician also "know himself"? Time and events alone will tell us whether Nixon has correctly "analyzed" his American Dream, or whether a deeper interpretation would be better for the health and well-being of America and the world.

# 6

# THE PSYCHO-HISTORICAL APPROACH

★★★★★★★★★★★★★★★★★★★★★★★★★★★★★★★★★★★★★★★★★★

**W**HAT exactly is the psychohistorical approach and how have we used it to help us to understand a public figure such as Richard Nixon? Pioneered by Freud in his study of Leonardo da Vinci, psychohistory has manifested itself mainly as psychobiography and has generally emphasized the psychoanalytic rather than the historical side of the equation. Moreover, psychohistory has too frequently used early id- and sex-oriented psychoanalytic theory, which Freud himself eventually went beyond, in order to stress the ego and more mature cognitive processes as well. In this light the definition of psychohistory as the application of psychoanalysis to history is *too* simple, and we must add to our definition.

Psychohistory is the application to history in general, as well as to specific historical figures, of a particular kind of psychoanalytic theory, one that emphasizes ego and superego as well as id factors, and that pays special attention to defensive and adaptive mechanisms. On the other hand (and just as importantly), it seeks to apply history to psychoanalysis—that is, to re-examine psychoanalytical concepts in the light of historical change. For example, while all children presumably experience an Oedipal conflict of sorts—it is a universal constant in this sense—the particular way it is experienced and its intensity vary enormously in different times and cultures. To take one factor, changes in diet may affect the onset of puberty (which can occur as early as age twelve or as late as seventeen). Changes in educational opportunity may affect the cultural context in which a reawakened Oedipal conflict can arise. In short, the psychoanalytic concept of an Oedipal complex takes on new meaning when the history surrounding it is examined.

In the case of Richard Nixon, as we have seen, his relations

with his mother, father, and siblings could not readily be analyzed in terms of classic psychoanalytic theory about the Oedipal
complex, even if we had wished to do so (and we didn't). At
present at least, there is a lack of materials about his early childhood and adolescence. Yet we can assume that the *way* in which
he passed through his Oedipal phase—a necessary phase in the
development of all young men, for, without it, identification
with a model of a mature man would be hampered—was of
great importance and affected later relationships in his life. So,
too, because of lack of information, we cannot, in fact, tell how
typical his experiences were, but we can postulate, in theory,
a significant connection with his Quaker religion, his rural, Californian culture, his maturation in twentieth-century American
society, and so forth.

The above may sound complicated, and it is. Without my
going into further details, the reader can readily perceive how
numerous are the interactions among the psychoanalytic and
historical materials. Psychohistory is not *merely* the application
of psychoanalysis to history but a true fusion of the two, creat-
ing a new vision.

We must now discuss the limitations, or, to use a better if
more pretentious term, the boundary conditions surrounding this
new way of looking at things. The first point that needs to be
stressed is that psychohistory's conclusions, alas, cannot (or at
least should not) be presented in summary terms, without a
clear understanding that such a procedure is like saying that
Proust's *Remembrance of Things Past* is about a man reminiscing in bed, or *Hamlet* is about a young man who suspects his
kingly father has been poisoned by his uncle. When the *New
York Times* originally mentioned the article from which this
present book has grown, it was forced to pull out such quotes as
that Mr. Nixon "compensates for his lack of active abilities,
where this is the case, by enormous hard work and persistence,"
and that he has had a "serious problem with death wishes and
anxiety; in relation to his brothers, himself and Eisenhower."[1]

Clearly, any conviction that such statements may arouse in a reader can only come from the detailed supporting data behind them. It is the *density* of material, building up a conclusion as one builds up a puzzle, that makes such summary statements anything more than parlor-room Freudian clichés.

` As Freud remarked,

> If one succeeds in arranging the confused heap of fragments, each of which bears upon it an unintelligible piece of drawing, so that the picture acquires a meaning, so that there is no gap anywhere in the design and so that the whole fits into the frame—if all these conditions are fulfilled, then one knows that one has solved the puzzle and that there is no alternative solution.

Psychohistory, in short, cannot be reduced to mathematical formulas or simple lawlike statements, as the physical sciences can. Nor can psychohistory rest content with pseudostatements, or snap judgments, such as "Nixon is a depressive type" or "Nixon has a severe Oedipal complex, displaced on to his sibling rivals." Such statements by themselves, even if they were true, tell us little of value and are generally misleading.

Freud himself recognized the way in which psychoanalysis has to tease out its conclusions from a mass of detail, and at the end still remains embedded in that detail. Comparing psychoanalysis to archaeology (Freud's favorite hobby), he indicated the way in which the archaeologist, like the analyst, had to make sense out of bits and pieces of surviving materials. "If his work is crowned with success," Freud declared, "the discoveries are self-explanatory; the ruined walls are part of the ramparts of a palace or treasure house; the fragments of columns can be filled out into a temple; the numerous inscriptions, which, by good luck, may be bilingual, reveal an alphabet and a language, and, when they have been deciphered and translated, yield undreamed-of information about the events of the remote past, to commemorate which the monuments were built."

Thus, the whole gives meaning to the parts, just as the parts can be understood only in terms of the whole. Mr. Nixon's death wishes and anxieties are *his* wishes and anxieties, not abstract and generalized feelings, and are related to *his* specific lack of native abilities, *his* dreams and daydreams, and so forth. As in psychoanalysis per se, so in psychohistory; just as the whole puzzle gives meaning eventually, for example, to a fuzzy bit of green and brown, which, correctly placed, forms into part of a tree, so a death anxiety, rightly perceived, comes to form part of a total personality.

In relying on what I am calling "density" (which is, it must be added immediately, not mere agglomeration of data but their accumulation in a definite configuration) rather than on isolated and lawlike statements, psychoanalysis is much akin to history and its form of explanations. In fact, of course, psychoanalysis is a form of *personal* history. As Hans Meyerhoff has so well expressed it, both psychoanalysis and history deal with materials from the past, seek to "reconstruct" a pattern of events from fragmentary data, and offer an "explanation" based on the totality of this reconstruction rather than on general laws.[2]

Nevertheless, while sharing many of the characteristics of history, psychoanalysis differs from history in one fundamental way. It claims to have a scientific system of concepts, based on clinical data. This claim I accept. Before Freud and his followers, many deep-seeing people had intuitive glimpses into the human psyche. Pascal, Stendhal, Schopenhauer, Dostoevsky, and Nietzsche: one has only to mention such names to see how searing (if I may pun) has been the glance into what Freud called "an intellectual hell." What Freud added to their insights, as he himself constantly acknowledged, was system, and the grounding and regrounding of his systematized concepts in clinical evidence, and then the hard work of detailed analysis of particular case "histories," which in turn provided new concepts.

Such a conceptualized system offers advantages unavailable to poetic intuition. Intuition may result in flashes of insight into a character such as Nixon's. But it cannot steadily and

154

constantly provide us with questions to raise about him (or any other such subject)—questions, for example, about how Nixon handles anxieties of various sorts, such as the threat of passivity or failure, about what his characteristic defenses are (projection, displacement, and so forth) and how compulsively he uses them, and on and on in the technical vocabulary of psychoanalysis. The psychoanalytic system of concepts also allows for certain kinds of verification denied to mere intuition, as when it appeals to the concerted evidence of slips, dreams, free association, symbol interpretation, content analysis, and so forth. In addition, psychoanalysis allows us to relate our insights (which may, of course, be initially derived from pure intuition), one to another—that, after all, is what is meant by its being a systematic science—and, especially important, to relate them dynamically, that is, as describing an ongoing process rather than merely serving as a classification. We can study not only Nixon's projections—merely classifying them under some technical name would not be too helpful—but the way in which he uses them and the functions that they serve both personally and politically. All of this is possible because of the systemized, scientific nature of Freudian psychoanalysis, as it leads to psychohistory.

This is not, however, the place to go into the details of Freud's work in theoretical terms. For our purposes here, we need only repeat that in using psychoanalysis the psychohistorian is employing a scientifically conceptualized approach to certain materials, an approach that is foreign to the nature of history itself in the sense, as we have already suggested, that history is a basically "unlawlike" discipline. This fact leaves psychohistory in a peculiar position. It seeks systematically to use the theories and concepts of a "science," psychoanalysis, to re-examine and "test" these same theories and concepts in terms of changing historical contexts, and yet, at the end, to offer an "explanation" that is more like general history than psychoanalytic science. In short, psychohistory is still a form of history.

\*   \*   \*

Psychohistory does not substitute for other ways of explaining the same phenomena; rather, it supplements such explanations, adding another dimension to the more common political or sociological analyses. Thus, for example, in his excellent book, *Nixon Agonistes,* Garry Wills offers a primarily ideological explanation.[3] His thesis is that Nixon is the last stand of traditional American liberalism, that his career and his politics represent the "crisis of the self-made man." In working out his thesis, Wills establishes a picture of Nixon, which, itself touched with sharp psychological acumen, allows us, if we are successful, to add our more deeply etched tones to form a composite portrait.

This "supplementary" character of psychohistory accords with its need to relate individual personality to the social context that helps shape it and that in turn is affected by the actions of the individual. Naturally, Nixon's decisions are ideological decisions, just as they are also decisions affected by political necessity, considerations of friendship, public opinion, and so on. But ideology is not something held totally separate from personality needs; the two are conjoined in one complex, functioning human being—in this case the President of the United States.

In this context it is useful to turn to the work of Erik H. Erikson, for, in dealing with an individual life history, Erikson has argued persuasively for what he calls coexisting or corresponding processes. By this he means that developments in the somatic processes, for example, body growth, affect and are affected by developments in ego processes (conscious learning and mastery of reality problems) and developments in superego processes (put simply, the realm of conscience and morality). As a gross example, an infant born crippled (somatic) will have difficulty learning to walk at the appropriate age level and will thus have a problem of "autonomy" (ego mastery) that will be complicated or made easier by the way in which his society treats its cripples (social context). Thus, when we analyze an individual such as Nixon, ideally we ought to study his development in these corresponding terms.

In similar fashion we can think of developments in the mature individual corresponding with developments in the political or economic area surrounding him. His psyche, developed in terms of earlier somatic, ego, and superego processes, will lead him to perceive events around him in a certain way, thus affecting those events themselves (especially if he is a leader). The political and economic developments will in turn affect the further development of his psyche, for such changes continue into maturity, though rooted in earlier, infantile developments.

Moreover, in order to know what is specific, and intensely personal, to a given political leader such as Nixon, one must also have a fairly good sense of what is common and public to all or most political figures. Thus, Nixon, as we have seen, thinks unusually well of himself. Does this intense narcissism border on megalomania, or is it absolutely normal behavior for almost all politicians? If the latter is true (as I suspect), does this suggest that a certain kind of personality tends to enter politics? Does this not also say something about us, the American voters, that we tend to approve and reward mainly this sort of political person? Here is a situation in which one factor exists in a corresponding relation to another factor. In this double sense of studying corresponding processes in the individual and between the individual and his society, we must proceed in the practice of psychohistory. Or, as we first put it, psychohistory cannot exist separated from other studies; it supplements but does not substitute for other kinds of inquiries.

This leads us to our next point. Just as psychohistory does not eliminate the need for other inquiries—quite the contrary— so it cannot merely reduce its subject to the status of a patient.

157

Reductionism, wherein a great political figure (Freud-Bullitt's Wilson?) is stripped down to his oral, anal, and genital aspects, divorced from the social context, and made into a purely pathological clinical specimen, is a great danger in applying psychoanalysis to history. A political leader is necessarily far more than the sum of his childish hangups.

Fortunately, the threat of reductionism is itself often reduced accidentally by the absence of documentary material on a political leader's early life. This is certainly the case with Nixon. What we know of his mother and father, brothers, childhood, and friends is fairly superficial. Impressions about Nixon's childhood are relatively untrustworthy. Worse, we have few hints as to what sorts of responses—identifications, reaction formations—the reality of his family circle, even if we could establish that reality, actually elicited from Richard Nixon. Unlike Gandhi, for example, he has not written an autobiography, which would give us at least a version of his psychic reality, that is, the way *he* perceived external circumstances and reacted to them. We can only guess at these matters from his later patterns of behavior, and we must be careful in our guess.

Where possible, of course, we must make every effort to get at the actuality, and not just the psychic reality. For example, the evidence seems clear that Nixon's father did, in fact, have a violent temper. As a child Nixon was clearly aware of his father's irascibility. Now if Nixon had only *perceived* his father as having a temper—that is, had a childish fantasy, perhaps out of a bad conscience—this would have one meaning for the psychohistorian. If the father actually had such a temper (as he did), this suggests a different meaning. The psychohistorian must constantly seek to establish the facts—a difficult task in any sort of history—as best he can, and to be especially aware that his enterprise is most difficult in relation to childhood experiences. Reductionism, therefore, at best is methodologically invidious, and at worst is built on quicksand.

\*    \*    \*

We must now deal with a related point. It is frequently asserted that psychohistory is impossible because its subjects are beyond the reach of the analyst; either they are dead, or, if living, they are unavailable for true analysis. If the aim were therapy, this would undoubtedly be true. But if the aim is psychoanalytic understanding of a personality, then surely it depends on the amount of available material; where there is little or no pertinent material, psychohistorical inquiry obviously ought not to be attempted. (Incidentally, it might be remarked that a patient who will not speak or go to an analyst is also a hopeless enterprise—a not unfamiliar clinical experience.) As the political scientist Alexander George has pointed out, the clinician's ability to question his patient is limited to the patient's response. There is almost no way of verifying the patient's picture of himself and the world around him: all the clinical analyst can have, more or less, is "psychic reality" as presented by the patient. The psychohistorian, on the other hand, will, if lucky, have a mass of relevant material: family, friends, and enemies. The result is a check, and double check, on the psychohistorian's interpretation of the general character pattern of his subject from outside sources. Moreover, since he is interested in psychohistorical understanding and not therapy, the historian will usually not be concerned with certain kinds of intimate data that might be missing from the written record. (In any case he will not have the immediate experiential data, the affect brought into the open by transference, which is attached to such facts.) All in all, in terms of validity there is no reason to abandon hope for psychohistory: quite the opposite.

As for validation and verification of a particular analysis, this is immeasurably aided by a special aspect of psychoanalysis itself: the phenomenon of overdetermination. The problem of determinism in psychoanalysis bothers its unsympathetic critics. Freud insisted that strict determinism prevailed in psychic acts; there are no "accidents." "Free association," the basis of dream analysis and therapy, is "free" only in the sense that it is not hampered by the censorship of "logical," "rational" thought and mores. It is not, however, undetermined.

In fact, like almost all other processes in psychoanalysis, free association is overdetermined. That is, on the one hand, the same word or symbol may refer to many elements in a person's unconscious, while, on the other, a single unconscious drive or behavior process can give rise to innumerable conscious manifestations. To illustrate the first side of overdetermination, we may cite Freud's example of his dream of a Botanical Monograph. In this dream, as he tells us, the botanical component "led by numerous connecting paths deeper and deeper into the tangle of dream-thoughts. 'Botanical' was related to the figure of Professor *Gartner* [Gardener], the *blooming* looks of his wife to my patient *Flora* and to the lady (Frau L.) of whom I had told the story of the forgotten *flowers*. . . . A train of thought joined the lady with the flowers to my wife's *favourite flowers* and thence to the title of the monograph which I had seen for a moment during the day." As Freud concludes, "each of the elements of the dream's content turns out to have been 'overdetermined'—to have been represented in the dream-thoughts many times over." As we shall see in the course of our own work, representation "many times over" can occur not only in dreams, but in other products of thought such as in letters, speeches, autobiographical accounts, and the like.

To understand the second side of overdetermination, take, for example, possible castration anxiety. Such anxiety might manifest itself by an infatuation with the Medusa head (as analyzed by Freud, and as exhibited by Hitler), by an unusual interest in decapitations, by an excessive fascination with Henry VIII and the execution of his wives, and so forth. In short, the single anxiety can manifest itself in multiple ways.

Because of overdetermination, the psychohistorian can hope for abundant evidence on the meaning and significance of a particular element—say, the use of the term "botanical" and its connected images—as well as for numerous representations of a concern by his subject with, for example, anality, castration, Oedipal conflict, and so forth. Such evidence, moreover, becomes self-confirming in the sense that, as he proceeds, the psychohistorian can see whether additional or similar evidence is forthcoming.

When the fact of overdetermination is placed next to the frequent existence of outside observations—by family or friends —we find ourselves quite comfortably ensconced in the historian's traditional task of reconciling and interpreting conflicting and confirming evidence. The only difference in psychohistory is that the interpretation and confirmation of evidence must be done with an informed awareness of the meaning and application of psychoanalytic theory. But, what would one expect?

Can psychohistory be used for prediction? This is the next point we must examine critically. Both history and psychoanalysis are fundamentally "retrodictive" inquiries. By this we mean that they generally start from a given event, a "presenting situation"—an hysterical patient, a world war, and so forth— and then seek to explain how it came about and *what it means.* As Freud candidly confessed in relation to psychoanalysis, one cannot predict how a patient will behave in the future because "we never know beforehand which of the determining factors will prove the weaker or the stronger." "So long," he continued, "as we trace the development from its final outcome backwards, the chain of events appears continuous, and we feel we have gained an insight which is completely satisfactory backwards, the chain of events appears continuous, and we start from the premises inferred from the analysis and try to follow these up to the final result, then we no longer get the impression of an inevitable sequence of events which could not have been otherwise determined." At the end we can only say "that those [determining factors] which succeeded must have been the stronger." To this the historian in his own work can only say "Amen."

The determining causes are so varied, and so indeterminate in their strengths, that, whatever the situation in theory, in practice we can never predict with certainty. What we can do is twofold: indicate a pattern and extrapolate from it; and explain what the data mean. At the end, hopefully, we are able to exclaim: "Ah, now I understand," though the understanding is not of the sort involved in the Second Law of Thermodynamics.

Do we also say, "Ah, now I see," with the overtones of "Ah, now I also foresee"? I think we do to a limited extent. When Mr. Nixon, in his book *Six Crises,* referred to his opponents in a particular context as "bums" and then applied the term to student demonstrators, I, at least, felt that I had been there before (and tried to explain why in this book). What I was "predicting" was that "bums" meant something special in Nixon's psychic economy, and that under certain special conditions it was likely to appear as a term of opprobrium.

Yet this is not quite the same thing as true prediction, and the distinction is a keen one. If, as in the natural sciences, the psychohistorian could state with utter certainty that Nixon's personality would compel him to keep Agnew as his Vice President in 1972, that would be "true prediction." Such true prediction, however, is not possible in psychohistory.

Nevertheless, the temptation to predict is great, and political observers do it constantly and casually all the time. In his *Richard Nixon: A Political and Personal Portrait,* Earl Mazo predicted without qualification that Nixon, if elected, "would have a strong Secretary of State, one who could best fit the mold of Dulles, whom he esteems."[4] Whatever Nixon would have done in 1960, he certainly did not appoint a strong Secretary of State in 1968, when he put his old friend William Rogers in charge of the State Department. Perhaps, however, Mazo can be forgiven when we remember that Nixon himself wrote in

1961, in *Six Crises,* that the Vice President should be chosen, not on political or geographical considerations, but because he had the qualifications to take over the Presidency—and then, as we have noted, chose Spiro Agnew in 1968!

Walter Lippmann takes a more agnostic position on predictive possibilities, one with which I in large part agree. He observed at the beginning of Mr. Nixon's term that:

> In these early days of the Nixon Administration it has not been possible for anyone to forecast what is going to happen in the next four years. This is not surprising.
>
> No newspaperman that I can think of foresaw on Inauguration Day what Herbert Hoover or Franklin Roosevelt or John Kennedy or Lyndon Johnson would actually do. There is no binding connection between the words of a candidate in the campaign and the acts of the President when he is in the White House.
>
> Franklin Roosevelt's last campaign speech was an emphatic repetition of what President Hoover had been saying and had nothing to do with what he later did.
>
> From what Lyndon Johnson said about Vietnam in his campaign of 1964, it was impossible to foresee that a few months later he would begin to ruin himself in Vietnam.
>
> So I do not know what President Nixon will do. But I have a strong belief about what the actual situation of the United States demands of him.[5]

For Lippmann "the actual situation of the United States" is deflationary, especially in the area of foreign policy. But, true to his own admonitions, Lippmann does not attempt to predict how Nixon's personality will affect his behavior in such a situation.

However, another scholar, whom I also respect highly, James David Barber, who forgoes the Mazo-type of intuitive prediction in favor of a systematic approach, is more sanguine on the matter of exact prediction than either Lippmann or I. As a political scientist, he wishes to develop a model of Presidential behavior with strong predictive qualities. Working out a "Paradigm of Accentuations" and a classification of character on a

passive-active, positive-negative axis, Barber has applied his
schema to a number of Presidents, including Richard Nixon.
He claims that "in the hope of improving our predictions about
Presidents, it is worth trying to discern the key regularities.
This may bring us to the point where we can look over a field
of candidates and say, with a confidence beyond common sense,
where the main problems and possibilities are likely to lie."[6]
He classifies Nixon as active-negative and believes that the
general pattern of his future behavior will conform to this
classification.

Although gifted with psychological insight, Barber does not
explicitly use psychoanalysis, a dynamic approach. Nor does he
try to situate his prediction of Presidential behavior in an
historical context, deflationary or otherwise. There does exist,
however, one classic psychoanalytic study of a political leader,
which seeks to predict his likely behavior in various possible
situations. Unfortunately, it has never been published* and
until 1968 still bore a "secret" classification on its manila cover.
Prepared in 1943 for the Office of Strategic Services (America's
major intelligence service during World War II), it is a study of
Adolf Hitler by Dr. Walter Langer, a practicing analyst. Dr.
Langer shows a sharp historical awareness, perhaps honed to
a fine point by his relationship with his brother, the eminent
diplomatic historian, William Langer. Written long before the
advent of psychohistory as a defined field, this pioneering study
employs classical, orthodox psychoanalysis in an inspired manner to give us a portrait in depth of Adolf Hitler. Dr. Langer
then posits various political eventualities for Germany in the
war and advances an educated prediction as to how Hitler
would behave in the circumstances. Dr. Langer's predictions
have an uncanny accuracy.

Even with such encouragement to prediction, however, I still
wish to stress how tremulous an enterprise it is for psychohistory.

* It will be published by Basic Books in the fall of 1972.

The Psychohistorical Approach

The Langer study is a sort of happy accident. After all, in 1943 only a limited number of situational choices were still open to its subject, Hitler, and therefore various boundary conditions could be realistically postulated. So, too, Barber's system does not leave me convinced that it will yield what I have called "true prediction." As Lippmann suggests, it could not have predicted FDR's policy, although it might have suggested a possible behavior pattern—pragmatism, for example—on the part of the President in 1933.

In short, I am forced to repeat that psychohistory is basically a retrospective inquiry. Glancing backwards, one can then cast a look into the future, which may carry some light glowing luminously from the past. Understanding Nixon's past actions should give us greater confidence in speculating about his future behavior, but it cannot give us the sort of certainty involved in true prediction. Above all, it cannot forecast a specific act, such as visiting Peking.

Let us try to sum up what we have said about psychohistory. We have defined it as a *fusion* of psychoanalysis and history (not a mere application of one to the other) in which both disciplines modify the other. (This is the ideal; in practice, as yet, history has had too little to say about the psychoanalytic concepts.) The findings of psychohistory cannot readily and profitably be summarized; conviction comes from the *density*, in configurational form, of confirming evidence. The findings themselves are essentially retrodictive and only in very small part can be made predictive; what psychohistory primarily offers is increased understanding of the meaning and significance of its materials. Moreover, in its findings psychohistory is presenting supplementary material and hypotheses, not substitutes for other endeavors in the social or political sciences. It accomplishes this by focusing on what I have called "corresponding processes." Lastly, it must avoid falling into the abyss of reductionism and concentrating on the data of infancy. Its subjects are mature, functioning people and must be treated as such. Fortunately, sufficient, and sometimes abundant data, made more convincing by the phenomenon of overdeterminism, can usually be found for the adult behavior of outstanding leaders.

In the light of these assertions we can justify our effort to look at Richard Nixon in psychohistorical terms. In this book we have been looking at Nixon's fundamental patterns of feeling and behavior, tracing their rise chronologically where we could. As we examined his relations with his mother, his siblings, and his father, we sought to understand the strong role played by death in his family. His religious beliefs and their relations to his feelings about authority; the rural-urban split in his attachments and his ambivalence about the Eastern Establishment; his daydreaming, loneliness, and introspection; his lawyer-politician ambitions; his romantic courtships; his propensity for dramatics and for debating; his projections; his identification of personal with national interest; his crises and the letdown feeling they bring; and his relations with Eisenhower: all these, and more, figured in our psychohistorical analysis. So, too, we needed to investigate Nixon's self-image, the role in his psychic economy of passivity and compassion, and Nixon's oral and anal images and modes of dealing with people and things. Finally, in the last chapter, we tested our analysis by applying it to recent crises—specifically, the Haynsworth-Carswell nominations, the Cambodian invasion, the decision to visit Peking, and the reversal of economic policy—and then sought a final answer to the question whether we are in the presence of a "new" Nixon, and what our answer means for America. All of these topics we have dealt with in the spirit of psychohistory as we have tried to define it up to now.

Earlier we acknowledged that many people are wary of applying psychoanalysis to historical figures (and usually distrust therapy as well, a problem with which we cannot deal here). Yet few people seem to object to truly amateur non-psychoanalytic seat-of-the pants efforts to understand personality as it affects politics. We *all* resort unthinkingly to superficial comments of a psychoanalytic nature. For example, the very shrewd policy analyst Zbigniew Brzezinski in "Half Past Nixon," a fine article assessing Nixon's foreign policy halfway through his first term, talks of a "*subconscious* bureaucratic vested interest in the maintenance of a variety of political and military commitments" and of the importance of "psychological intangibles."[7] Why not explore the "psychological intangibles" penetratingly, cautiously, and carefully? Surely, the use of psychoanalysis in such an explanation promises more and deeper insights into these important areas than unsystematic and purely intuitive "hunches" (though these certainly have their rightful place).

Assuming psychohistory to be a valid enterprise, is it wrong to apply it to a living President? There is a beautiful line in Shakespeare where he talks about "the divinity that doth hedge a king." Ought one to question such "divinity"? Is political power based on faith and belief to such an extent that shaking these shakes, so to speak, the throne?

A political leader requires an aura of legitimacy, even if this is only his personal charisma. His rule rests ultimately on our consent, and this consent is best obtained if, in addition to the physical force (itself based on consent, once removed) at his disposal, we believe in his right to rule us. Moreover, a good leader satisfies our longing for being a part of a larger entity, part of a moral quest, a "crusade." "The President," James David Barber reminds us, "is expected to personify our betterness in an inspiring way, to express in what he does and is (not just in what he says) a moral idealism which, in much of the public mind, is the very opposite of politics."[8]

With this said, however, we must also remember that Americans have rejected kings and, therefore, the "divinity" surrounding them. In 1776 the basic decision was made to struggle for a polity founded in the light of reason, rather than of superstitious awe. We accepted Washington as a metaphoric "Father of his country," while rejecting kingly fathers. Yet as free, independent men, we reserved to ourselves the right to respect our political "father figures," without rendering them unquestioning, childish obedience.

Thus, the effort to understand "what kind of a human being" is the possessor of Presidential power takes on, not only its own legitimacy, but a certain urgency. Indeed, the propriety of such an inquiry in depth has already been established by sober, sensitive political observers, who, without using psychoanalysis, make their own psychological analyses of Mr. Nixon. To take but one example among many, consider Max Frankel's discussion of the President's decision to invade the enemy sanctuaries in Cambodia. "Perhaps," Frankel comments, "only the President knows the whole story, for it may turn as much on psychological as on tactical considerations." He continues:

Mr. Nixon has long been beset by fears that he would be found wanting by an antagonist in this nuclear age. Some of his advisers have expressed anxiety—as did their predecessors in the Johnson Administration—that division and dissension at home would be misread as weakness.

President Nixon had gone longer into his term of office than either President Kennedy or President Johnson without some militant demonstration of his resolve to act strongly abroad. When confronted with the news of the Vietnamese Communist action in the face of his withdrawal commitment, that deep need to draw the line at what he called the intolerable appears to have played itself out, in unknown measure.[9]

"That deep need." Here is a very dramatic way of underscoring the inseparability of personality and politics. Indeed, there is much good evidence that we vote for a "person," at least as often as we do for a "program," or "on the issues." Issues are generally vague and confused. Moreover, there are many issues, and not all the ones we favor are bound up with a particular candidate. Thus, we tend to vote on an "I like Ike" basis, rather than for or against his "policies." Or, rather, in a deep folk wisdom we may realize that his policies are bound up with his personality (alas, we may be misled in our intuitions, which is another argument for psychohistory).

Knowing this fact of political life, politicians frequently engage in gentle character assassination. Sometimes, they even descend into the gutter. In the past, perhaps out of lack of knowledge, they have stayed away from snide remarks on "deep needs." But nowadays, occasionally, they may even resort to such remarks, made for political advantage, as in the allegations about Goldwater's mental stability or Nixon's "therapy." These particular remarks came from the Democratic side, but the Republicans, too, are not above this sort of play when it is to their advantage. Thus, a recent news despatch reports that:

The Republican National Committee said yesterday that Senator Edmund S. Muskie's "short fuse" temper would be a factor in the 1972 race for President.

"While most of the media has portrayed Senator Muskie as calm, cool, and collected, those who have closely observed the Maine Democrat say that he is really a man with a very short fuse, ready to explode on a moment's notice," the committee said in its weekly publication.

The committee said the report was based on "articles by several political writers, a book on Muskie, a television interview and even quotes from his sister."

"It is apparent that the Muskie temper will be a factor in the 1972 Democratic presidential sweepstakes," the GOP said.[10]

Psychohistory, as I conceive of it, is not concerned with *partisan* politics; that is its ideal. In practice, of course, there is no way of preventing someone from using it maliciously, for political advantage. This is true of all "knowledge"; it can be misused (consider the atom). Presumably, the true meaning of Senator Muskie's alleged temper might emerge from an in-depth study of him, just as President Nixon's reactions to crisis are more fully revealed in a study such as this one. By placing the reality in the full context of the man's personality, and making

169

clear its "real" meaning, good psychohistory might be its own best defense against misuse. Surely, Senator Goldwater in 1964 would have been better served by such an inquiry than by vague innuendoes and unanswerable accusations.

I have said that psychohistory is not concerned with *partisan* politics. That does not mean it is unconcerned with politics: quite the opposite. When dealing with a political figure, it (or at least the present writer) is intensely concerned with increasing understanding in order to help to secure a better society. Further, having once carried out the inquiry in as "value-free" a manner as possible, the psychohistorian has, I believe, a duty to use its results according to his own values.

With this credo in mind, I should like to make two declarations about my psychohistorical study of Mr. Nixon. The first is that, throughout what has preceded, my comments and findings have tried to reveal as much about us, the American people, we said earlier about the nature of psychohistory and its con- as they do about the President himself. This follows from what centration on corresponding processes.

The second declaration, for which I cannot present the full evidence here, is that "style" of politics may be vastly different among political leaders—for example, John F. Kennedy and Richard Nixon—while the "substance" of personality may be greatly alike. From different backgrounds and different life experiences, political figures may arrive at the same character traits of competitiveness, fear of softness, and so forth. The reason must be sought in the fact that they all emerge from the same mold of American values; in short, from the constant corresponding processes and the basic "character" of the American people, as it has been up to now. In my judgment political scientists have concentrated too frequently on style instead of substance. Only detailed examination of a number of our recent Presidents could substantiate the point I am making here. Yet it is crucial to bear it in mind as we reflect upon our inquiry into the "real" Richard Nixon.

# NOTES

## 1 THE NIXON PROBLEM

1. Tom Wicker, *New York Times Magazine,* January 19, 1969, p. 21.

2. Richard H. Rovere, *New York Times Magazine,* July 20, 1969, p. 4; my italics.

3. There is a growing literature in this field, most of it stemming from the pioneering work by Erik H. Erikson, *Childhood and Society* (New York, 1950). My own position is put forth in the introduction to Bruce Mazlish, ed., *Psychoanalysis and History* (New York, 1971, revised ed.), and "Clio on the Couch: Prolegomena to Psychohistory," *Encounter* 31 (1968): 46–54. Cf. Cushing Strout, "Ego Psychology and the Historian," *History and Theory* 7 (1968): 281–297.

4. Sigmund Freud and William Bullitt, *Thomas Woodrow Wilson: A Psychological Study* (Boston, 1967).

5. View expressed by Tovah Silver Marion in a letter to *The Boston Globe,* November 26, 1968.

6. Joe McGinniss, *The Selling of the President, 1968* (New York, 1969), pp. 100–101.

7. Stewart Alsop, *Nixon and Rockefeller: A Double Portrait* (Garden City, 1960), p. 226.

8. Dr. Arnold A. Hutschnecker, "The Mental Health of Our Leaders," *Look* 33 (July 15, 1969): 51–52.

9. Alsop, *Nixon and Rockefeller,* p. 219.

10. Alexander and Juliette George, *Woodrow Wilson and Colonel House* (New York, 1956).

11. A 1968 news release informs us that "the U.S. Information Agency has been circulating abroad a film of President-elect Richard Milhous Nixon which pictures him as an 'intellectual introvert not unlike' President Woodrow Wilson. The 24-minute film carried the endorsement of Nixon headquarters." Nixon himself has also frequently stressed his admiration for, and identification with, Wilson. However, the Georges' suggestion that Wilson's idealism masked strong personal aggressive needs might give one pause in making this particular comparison. For a good analysis of the Georges' view of psychohistory, see Fred I. Greenstein, *Personality and Politics* (Chicago, 1969), esp. ch. 3.

12. Erik H. Erikson, *Young Man Luther* (New York, 1962); Erik H. Erikson, *Gandhi's Truth: On the Origins of Militant Nonviolence* (New York, 1969).

## 2 FAMILY AND ROOTS

1. For a magisterial treatment of this problem, see Erik H. Erikson, "On the Nature of Psycho-Historical Evidence: In Search of Gandhi," *Daedalus* 97 (1968): 695–730.

2. William H. Homan, "The Men Behind Nixon's Speeches," *New York Times Magazine,* January 19, 1969.

3. Robert B. Semple, Jr., "Nixon's Presidency Is a Very Private Affair," *New York Times Magazine,* November 2, 1969, pp. 124, 126.

4. Mark Harris, *Mark the Glove Boy* (New York, 1964), pp. 34–35.

5. Gary Wills, *Nixon Agonistes* (New York, 1970), p. 164.

6. Earl Mazo and Stephen Hess, *Nixon: A Political Portrait* (New York, 1968), p. 15.

7. Ibid., p. 16.

8. Ibid., p. 18.

9. Ibid., pp. 16–17.

10. See also William Costello, *The Facts about Nixon: An Unauthorized Biography* (New York, 1960), p. 23, for details.

11. James Keogh, *This Is Nixon* (New York, 1956), p. 25.

12. Donald Jackson, "The Young Nixon," *Life,* November 6, 1970.

13. Lloyd Shearer, *Boston Sunday Globe, Parade,* June 28, 1970, p. 7.

14. Richard Nixon, "My Brother, Arthur R. Nixon," reprinted in Bela Kornitzer, *The Real Nixon: An Intimate Biography* (New York, 1960), p. 64.

15. Richard Nixon, *Six Crises* (New York: Doubleday, 1968), p. 341; my italics.

16. Nixon, "My Brother, Arthur R. Nixon."

17. Ibid., p. 65.

18. George Johnson, *Richard Nixon* (Derby, 1961), p. 20.

19. Nixon, "My Brother, Arthur R. Nixon," p. 65; my italics.

20. See, for example, Robert Lifton, "On Death and Death Symbolism" and "The Hiroshima Bomb," reprinted in *History and Human Survival* (New York, 1970), and *Death in Life: Survivors of Hiroshima* (New York, 1967).

21. Mazo and Hess, *Nixon,* p. 13.

22. Costello, *Facts about Nixon,* p. 21.

23. "The Young Nixon," p. 60.

24. Kornitzer, *The Real Nixon,* p. 79.

25. Wills, *Nixon Agonistes,* p. 170.

26. Mazo and Hess, *Nixon,* p. 11.

27. Nixon, *Six Crises,* p. 312, my italics.

28. Ibid., p. 318.

29. Cf. Edward Fiske's article in the *New York Times,* January 26, 1969, p. 54.

30. Mazo and Hess, *Nixon,* p. 17.

31. American Friends Service Committee, *Who Shall Live?* (New York, 1970).

32. Wills, *Nixon Agonistes,* p. 32.

33. Ibid., p. 431.

34. *New York Times Magazine,* June 8, 1969, p. 108.

35. Ibid., p. 111.

36. Mazo and Hess, *Nixon,* p. 10.

37. "Billy Graham's Own Story: 'God Is My Witness,' Part One," *McCall's,* April 1964, p. 124. Cf. John Pollock, *Billy Graham: The Authorized Biography* (London, 1966), p. 18.

38. Kornitzer, *The Real Nixon,* pp. 78–79.

39. Nixon, *Six Crises,* p. 24.

40. Ibid., pp. 3–4.

41. Ibid., p. 32.

42. Mazo and Hess, *Nixon,* p. 31.

43. Ibid., p. 22.

44. Nixon, *Six Crises,* p. xiv.

45. Theodore White, *The Making of a President, 1968* (New York, 1969), p. 465.

46. Theodore White, *The Making of a President, 1960* (New York, 1961), p. 302.

47. Wills, *Nixon Agonistes,* p. 67.

48. Ibid., p. 159.

49. Ibid., p. 263.

50. Nixon, *Six Crises,* p. 19.

51. Ibid., p. 7.

52. Mazo and Hess, *Nixon,* p. 48.

53. Ibid., p. 52.

54. See Ibid., p. 258, for a beginning analysis, as well as Wills, *Nixon Agonistes,* pp. 75 ff.

55. Marie Smith, "Nixon's California Home," *Boston Globe,* July 6, 1969.

56. Mazo and Hess, *Nixon,* p. 10.

57. Wills, *Nixon Agonistes,* p. 174.

58. Semple, "Nixon's Presidency Is a Very Private Affair," p. 128.

59. White, *Making of President, 1960,* p. 358.

60. White, *Making of President, 1968,* p. 514.

61. Robert B. Semple, Jr., "The Three Strategies of a Master Politician," *New York Times Magazine,* November 1, 1970, p. 42.

## 3 YOUTH AND MATURITY

1. Mazo and Hess, *Nixon,* pp. 18–19.

2. Ibid., p. 30.

3. See, for example, Harold D. Lasswell, *Psychopathology and Politics* (Chicago, 1930).

4. Mazo and Hess, *Nixon,* p. 30.

5. Ibid., p. 33.

6. Nixon, *Six Crises,* p. 115.

7. Mazo and Hess, *Nixon,* p. 10.

8. Kornitzer, *The Real Nixon,* p. 46.

9. Nixon, *Six Crises,* p. 317.

10. Ibid.

11. Ibid., p. xv.

12. Ibid., pp. xv–xvi.

13. Ibid., p. xvi.

14. Kornitzer, *The Real Nixon,* p. 46.

15. Wills, *Nixon Agonistes,* p. 170.

16. Ibid., p. 173.

17. Robert B. Semple, Jr., "Nixon's Presidency Is a Very Private Affair," p. 128.

18. White, *Making of President, 1960,* p. 81.

19. Kornitzer, *The Real Nixon,* p. 53.

20. White, *Making of President, 1968,* p. 177; my italics.

21. White, *Making of President, 1960,* p. 81.

22. Keogh, *This Is Nixon,* pp. 19–21.

23. Mazo and Hess, *Nixon,* p. 32.

24. Ibid., pp. 32–33.

25. Lawrence F. Schiff, "Dynamic Young Fogies—Rebels on the Right," *Trans-Action* 4 (November 1966), p. 32.

26. Ibid.

27. White, *Making of President, 1968,* p. 183.

28. Semple, "Nixon's Presidency Is a Very Private Affair," p. 127.

29. Mazo and Hess, *Nixon,* p. 26.

30. Lloyd Shearer, *Boston Sunday Globe, Parade,* June 28, 1970.

31. Ibid., p. 5.

32. Mazo and Hess, *Nixon,* p. 26.

33. Ibid., p. 27.

34. Ibid., p. 29.

35. Costello, *Facts about Nixon,* p. 20.

36. Kornitzer, *The Real Nixon,* p. 33.

37. Nixon, *Six Crises,* p. 120.

38. Ibid., p. 404.

39. Wills, *Nixon Agonistes,* p. 30.

40. Ibid., pp. 178–179.

41. *New York Times,* March 14, 1971.

42. Mazo and Hess, *Nixon,* p. 19.

43. Ibid., p. 109.

44. Ibid., p. 120.

45. Ibid., p. 123.
46. Nixon, *Six Crises,* p. 132.
47. Ibid., p. xxvii.
48. Mazo and Hess, *Nixon,* pp. 51–52.
49. Ibid., pp. 45–46; my italics.
50. Ibid., p. 48; my italics.
51. Ibid., p. 52; my italics.
52. Ibid., p. 120.
53. Ibid., pp. 137–138.
54. Nixon, *Six Crises,* p. 271; my italics.
55. Ibid., pp. 299–300.
56. Ibid., p. 326; my italics.
57. Ibid., p. 137.
58. Jules Witcover, *The Resurrection of Richard Nixon* (New York, 1970), p. 135.
59. Wills, *Nixon Agonistes,* p. 406.
60. White, *Making of President, 1968,* p. 166.
61. Ibid., p. 538.
62. Mazo and Hess, *Nixon,* p. 39.
63. Ibid., pp. 234–235.
64. Nixon, *Six Crises,* p. 348; my italics.
65. White, *Making of President, 1960,* p. 326.
66. Ibid., pp. 344–345.
67. Mazo and Hess, *Nixon,* pp. 281–282.

## 4 PERSONAL CRISES IN A POLITICAL SETTING

1. Mazo and Hess, *Nixon,* p. 103.
2. Ibid., pp. 39, 40.
3. Ibid., pp. 40, 41.
4. Ibid., p. 65.
5. Nixon, *Six Crises,* p. 223.
6. Ibid., p. 235; my italics.
7. Mazo and Hess, *Nixon,* p. 177; my italics.
8. Nixon, *Six Crises,* p. 311.
9. Mazo and Hess, *Nixon,* p. 59.
10. See T. Adorno et al., *The Authoritarian Personality* (New York, 1950).
11. Cf. Richard Hofstadter, *The Paranoid Style in American Politics and Other Essays* (New York, 1965).
12. Mazo and Hess, *Nixon,* p. 62.
13. Nixon, *Six Crises,* pp. 2, 3, 4.
14. Mazo and Hess, *Nixon,* p. 137.
15. Ibid., p. 66.

16. Nixon, *Six Crises,* p. 312.
17. Mazo and Hess, *Nixon,* p. 312.
18. Ibid., p. 316.
19. Nixon, *Six Crises,* p. 15.
20. Ibid., p. 24.
21. Ibid., p. 40.
22. Ibid., p. 102.
23. Earl Mazo, *Richard Nixon: A Political and Personal Portrait* (New York, 1959), pp. 285–286.
24. Nixon, *Six Crises,* p. 12.
25. Ibid., p. 264.
26. Ibid., p. 298.
27. Ibid., p. 344.
28. Ibid., p. v.
29. Ibid., p. 12.
30. Ibid., p. 13.
31. Ibid., p. xvii.
32. Ibid., p. xxii.
33. Ibid., p. xxiv.
34. Ibid., p. xxiii.
35. Ibid., pp. xxiv–xxv.
36. Ibid., pp. xxvi, xxvii.
37. Ibid., p. 40.
38. Ibid., pp. 40–41; my italics.
39. Ibid., p. 41.
40. Ibid., pp. 39–40; my italics.
41. Ibid., p. 249.
42. Ibid., p. 248.
43. Ibid., p. 253.
44. Ibid., p. 313.
45. Ibid., pp. 181–182.
46. Ibid., p. 461.
47. Ibid., p. 152.
48. Ibid., p. 166.
49. Ibid., p. 102.
50. Ibid.
51. Ibid., p. 116.
52. Ibid., p. 106.
53. Mazo and Hess, *Nixon,* p. 146.
54. Ibid., p. 183.
55. *New York Times,* May 1, 1970; my italics.
56. Lloyd Shearer, *Boston Sunday Globe, Parade,* June 28, 1970.
57. Mazo and Hess, *Nixon,* p. 16.
58. Nixon, *Six Crises,* pp. 260, 263.
59. Mazo and Hess, *Nixon,* p. 199.

60. Nixon, *Six Crises,* p. 304.
61. Ibid., p. 305.
62. Mazo and Hess, *Nixon,* p. 285.
63. Nixon, *Six Crises,* p. 98.
64. Ibid., p. 129.
65. Ibid., p. 81.
66. Ibid., p. 131.
67. Mazo and Hess, *Nixon,* p. 159.
68. Ibid., p. 110.
69. Cf. Wills, *Nixon Agonistes,* pp. 108ff.
70. Witcover, *The Resurrection of Richard Nixon,* p. 23.
71. Mazo and Hess, *Nixon,* p. 121.
72. Nixon, *Six Crises,* p. 167.
73. Ibid., p. 162.
74. Ibid., p. 163.
75. Mazo and Hess, *Nixon,* p. 145.
76. Nixon, *Six Crises,* pp. 171–172.
77. Ibid., p. 176.
78. Ibid.
79. Ibid., p. 178.
80. Mazo and Hess, *Nixon,* p. 238.
81. *New York Times,* February 1, 1970.

## 5 THE PRESIDENTIAL NIXON

1. Nixon, *Six Crises,* p. xxvi.
2. Mazo and Hess, *Nixon,* p. 228.
3. Nixon, *Six Crises,* p. 8; my italics.
4. Mazo and Hess, *Nixon,* p. 316.
5. Nixon, *Six Crises,* pp. 85–86.
6. Ibid., p. 152.
7. Ibid., p. 194.
8. Ibid., pp. 359–360.
9. Ibid., p. 382.
10. Ibid., pp. 382–383.
11. Ibid., p. 302.
12. Ibid., p. 273.
13. Mazo and Hess, *Nixon,* p. 132.
14. Nixon, *Six Crises,* p. 14.
15. Ibid., p. 367.
16. Wills, *Nixon Agonistes,* pp. 17–18.
17. White, *Making of President, 1968,* p. 161.
18. Wills, *Nixon Agonistes,* p. 493; my italics.
19. Costello, *Facts about Nixon,* p. 21.

20. Wills, *Nixon Agonistes*, p. 587.
21. White, *Making of President, 1960*, pp. 356–357.
22. Ibid., p. 77.
23. *Business Week*, July 31, 1971.
24. Semple, "Nixon's Presidency Is a Very Private Affair," p. 122.
25. Wills, *Nixon Agonistes*, p. 30.
26. White, *Making of President, 1968*, p. 400.
27. Mazo and Hess, *Nixon*, p. 17.
28. Kornitzer, *The Real Nixon*, p. 121.
29. Wills, *Nixon Agonistes*, p. 408.
30. Witcover, *Resurrection of Richard Nixon*, p. 22.
31. Earl Mazo, *Richard Nixon: A Political and Personal Portrait* (New York, 1959), p. 5.
32. Witcover, *Resurrection of Richard Nixon*, p. 140.
33. *New York Times*, April 12, 1970.
34. Quoted in *New York Times Book Review*, April 4, 1971, p. 3.
35. Witcover, *Resurrection of Richard Nixon*, p. 128.
36. Semple, "Nixon's Presidency Is a Very Private Affair," p. 128.
37. *New York Times Book Review*, April 4, 1971, p. 3; my italics.
38. *New York Times*, April 12, 1970.
39. *New York Times*, May 10, 1970.
40. *Boston Globe*, May 14, 1970.
41. *The Joint Appearances of Senator John F. Kennedy and Vice President Richard M. Nixon. Presidential Campaign of 1960* (U.S. Government Printing Office, Washington, 1961), p. 21.
42. Ibid., pp. 21–22.
43. Ibid., p. 7.
44. Ibid.
45. *New York Times*, May 1970.
46. *The Joint Appearances of Senator John F. Kennedy and Vice President Richard M. Nixon. Presidential Campaign of 1960* (U.S. Government Printing Office, Washington, 1961), p. 22.
47. Emmet John Hughes, "From the New Frontier to the New Revolution," *New York Times Magazine*, April 4, 1971, p. 25.
48. White, *Making of President, 1968*, p. 184.
49. Ibid., p. 317; my italics.
50. Ibid., pp. 515–516.
51. Ibid., p. 50; my italics.
52. *The Joint Appearances of Senator John F. Kennedy and Vice President Richard M. Nixon. Presidential Campaign of 1960* (U.S. Government Printing Office, Washington, 1961), p. 21.
53. Witcover, *Resurrection of Richard Nixon*, p. 212.
54. White, *Making of President, 1968*, p. 160.
55. Witcover, *Resurrection of Richard Nixon*, pp. 149–150; my italics.
56. Ibid., p. 151.

57. Quoted in *The Joint Appearances of Senator John F. Kennedy and Vice President Richard M. Nixon. Presidential Campaign of 1960* (U.S. Government Printing Office, Washington, 1961), p. 21.

58. Wills, *Nixon Agonistes,* p. 147.

59. Nixon, *Six Crises,* p. 460.

60. Mazo and Hess, *Nixon,* p. 253.

## 6 THE PSYCHOHISTORICAL APPROACH

1. *New York Times,* July 3, 1971.

2. See Hans Meyerhoff, "On Psychoanalysis and History," *Psychoanalysis and the Psychoanalytic Review* 49, no. 2 (Summer 1962).

3. Garry Wills, *Nixon Agonistes* (New York, 1970).

4. Earl Mazo, *Richard Nixon: A Political and Personal Portrait* (New York, 1959), p. 289.

5. *Boston Globe,* February 16, 1969.

6. *New York Times,* September 4, 1969.

7. Zbigniew Brzezinski, "Half Past Nixon," *Foreign Policy,* Summer 1971, pp. 4 and 18; my italics.

8. James David Barber, *New York Times,* September 4, 1969.

9. Max Frankel, *New York Times,* May 2, 1970.

10. *Boston Globe,* March 1, 1971.

# BIBLIOGRAPHY

Earl Mazo and Stephen Hess, *Nixon: A Political Portrait* (New York, 1968), is the rewrite of Earl Mazo, *Richard Nixon: A Political and Personal Portrait* (New York, 1959). For a comparison of the original book and the rewritten version, see the somewhat partisan and antagonistic review by Marvin Kitman in the *New York Times Book Review,* January 19, 1969. Seemingly the earliest book on Nixon is Philip Andrews, *This Man Nixon* (Philadelphia, 1952), only sixty-three pages, with some interesting photographs. In addition, there are James Keogh, *This Is Nixon* (New York, 1956), also with photographs; Ralph de Toledano, *Nixon* (New York, 1956), which is highly admiring of its subject; William A. Reuben, *The Honorable Mr. Nixon* (New York, 1958), which is a hostile account of Nixon's role in the Hiss case; Bela Kornitzer, *The Real Nixon: An Intimate Biography* (New York, 1960), which is replete with photographs, claims to be based on a number of taped interviews, and is about the only book on Nixon that openly states as its major interest Nixon's personality and family background, though it has some strange omissions; William Costello, *The Facts about Nixon: An Unauthorized Biography* (New York, 1960), which, while openly critical of Nixon, is a fairly substantial work; Stewart Alsop, *Nixon and Rockefeller: A Double Portrait* (Garden City, 1960), which emphasizes Nixon as politician; and George Johnson, *Richard Nixon* (Derby, 1961). What is striking about all of these books is their repetition, with variations that make one wonder who is being accurate, of exactly the same stories about Nixon, with no attribution of source that measures up to the standard with which a historian would feel comfortable. The only serious psychological study of Nixon is James David Barber's fine, interesting paper delivered at the 65th Annual Meeting of the American Political Science Association in September 1969, and published in a partial version as "Analyzing Presidents: From Passive-Positive Taft to Active-Negative Nixon," *Washington Monthly* I (October 1969): 33–54.

In addition to these works directly on Nixon, one might also consult such accounts of campaigns in which he was involved as Theodore White, *The Making of a President, 1960* (New York, 1961), and *The Making of a President, 1968* (New York, 1969); David English and the staff of the London *Daily Express, Divided They Stand* (New York, 1969); Joe McGinniss, *The Selling of the President, 1968* (New York, 1969); and so forth. An oral history project covering Nixon's early life is being

181

sponsored by Whittier College. In addition rumor has it that new books on Nixon are being written by Daniel P. Moynihan, Bryce Harlow, and Robert Semple, Jr., among others. (In fact, as this book was being prepared for the press, Rowland Evans, Jr. and Robert D. Novak's *Nixon in the White House* [New York, 1971] made its appearance, and Philip Roth's *Our Gang (Starring Tricky and His Friends)* [New York, November 1971], a new novel about a fictional Nixon, was published when this book was already in galleys.)

# INDEX

# Index

McCormick, Ken, 89
McCracken, Paul, 61
McGinniss, Joe, 6
Manson, Charles, 128
Marshall Plan, 81
Marshburn, Mrs. Olive, Richard Nixon's aunt, 43, 51, 54
Mazo, Earl, 68, 86, 162
Mazo, Earl and Hess, Stephen, 18, 19, 21, 37, 65, 77, 100, 114, 122; *Nixon: A Political Portrait,* 16
Meyerhoff, Hans, 154
Mitchell, John, 41, 116, 128, 129
More, Sir Thomas, 74
Moscow, Alvin, 18
Moynihan, Daniel Patrick, 120
Mudge, Stern (law firm), 38, 119
Muskie, Edmund S., 169

negative identity, 23, 96
New Economic Policy, 4, 120, 136ff.
Newlin, Professor, 7
new Nixon, a, 142ff.
Nietzsche, Friedrich, 154
Nixon, Arthur, 20, 21, 23, 24, 25, 26, death of, 25
Nixon, Donald, 19, 20, 21, 22, 24, 27, 28, 54
Nixon, Edward, 20
Nixon, Mrs. Francis A. (Hannah Milhous), 19, 20, 27, 30, 35, 67, 69, 122, 145
Nixon, Francis A. (Frank), 27, 28, 29, 30, 35, 55, 67, 69, 118
Nixon, Harold, 20, 21, 22, 25, 26, 122
Nixon, Julie (Mrs. David Eisenhower), 98, 105
Nixon Problem, the, 33ff.
Nixon, Richard: on abortion, 32, 33; acting, 70ff., 123; and aggression, 94, 96, 100, 103, 110, 123, 129, 132, 140, 146; ambivalence, 94, 97, 119, 138, 146; anality, 101, 102, 123, 124; and anticommunism, 82; authority, attitude to, 33ff., body rigidity, 124; bums, 95, 96, 115, 132, 162; California gubernatorial race,

94; Cambodian episode, 131ff., 135; career choice, 57; China policy, 135, 138ff., 141; and communism, 81, 83, 84, 85, 111, 131, 138; compassion, 119; conservatism, 60, 61; Constitution, strict construction of, 128, 130; control, need for, 124; courtships, 62ff., 66; crises, 76, 87, 88ff., 90, 91, 92, 104, 118, 122, 127, 136, 137, 138, 139, 140; daydreaming, 51, 116; death of brothers, 22; death fears, 26, 33, 132; death wishes, 125; as debater, 50ff., 76, 78, 123; decision-making, 56, 57; decisiveness, 93, 94, 118, 124, 132, 140; denial, as defense, 146; dependency, fear of, 118ff., 146; dramatics, 65; failure, threat of, 38, 130, 135, 142; family, 19ff.; father-figure, need for, 98, 103, 104, 125; football, 49; Haynsworth-Carswell crisis, 127ff., 135; illnesses, 49; indecisiveness, 94, 96, 127; intellectuals, attitude to, 40, 89, 90, 145; and internationalism, 81, introspection, 54; job hunt, 37; and Kent State, 132, 134, 135; lack of place, 44; as lawyer, 128; loneliness, 54, 56; mother's absence, 22; New Economic Policy, 136ff.; a new Nixon, 142ff.; oral aggression, 123; orality, 121ff., 123, 134, and paranoic fears, 84; passivity, 115ff., 146, 155; paucity of information on, 15, as peaceful man, 132, 141; populism, 40; pragmatism, 74, 85, 135, 141; as President, 109ff.; railroad ambitions, 28, 52, 74; religion, 31, 43; roles, 72, 73, 74, 75, 76, 146; and rural California, 37; rural values, 38; self-image, 109ff.; *Six Crises,* 18, 29, 76, 77, 87, 89, 110, 112, 162, 163; spankings, 34, 35; speeches, 17ff.; strength, admiration of, 116; in therapy, 6, 9, 169; traveling, 51; wage-price controls, 135, 136; warfare of poli-